(Rational) Animal

Casey Rentmeester

Published in the United States of America by Continuing Existence Press
PO Box 2512, Bloomington, Indiana 47401

Scuola di Atene (School of Athens), Raffaello Sanzio da Urbino (Raphael), 1509–1511, fresco, 200 in x 300 in, Apostolic Palace, Vatican Museums, Vatican City. Public Domain.

Library of Congress Cataloging-in-Publication Data
Rentmeester, Casey, 1983–
(Rational) Animal / Casey Rentmeester
ISBN 979-8-9941991-2-1

Contents

LIST OF FIGURES

Introduction
Timely Meditations

Humanity is immersed in confusion. We crown ourselves as the rational animal but have forgotten the *anima*—the breath that begets being and flows through the entirety of life on the planet. As such, we have severed our relationship with the rest of the natural world and forgotten our vital connection with it. Our confusion comes at a cost: anthropogenic—that is, *human*-created—climate change threatens the sustainability of human life as we have come to know it on this planet. Moreover, the Sixth Extinction is well underway: species are dying off at a rate that far exceeds the natural background extinction rate that would be evolutionarily explainable. We live, as philosopher Guy Debord recognized in 1971, on a sick planet. Disinterested leaders grip to power and control while our sociopolitical systems break down, our mental health suffers, and many of us can't help but sink into a helpless tone of nihilism. What is it all for? Why am I here? What is my proper place and purpose? Why do we treat each other this way?

Although the complexity of these questions is vast, nature itself can supply the answers to all of these questions in ways that are becoming increasingly apparent at an ethical and scientific level. Humanity, at its core, is nature rendered conscious in human form. Moreover, humanity is inextricably connected with all other living beings. We are individuals but never wholly individual. Although the great philosophical, spiritual, and religious traditions of the world differ in immensely important ways, there are similarities between them that we sometimes fail to acknowledge. Recognizing these similarities is crucial in uniting humanity and initiating a paradigm shift in the relationship between humanity and nature.

The human relationship with nature has been variously interpreted throughout the world's history—as our creative mother, as the source of life, or even as an unrelenting, indifferent force. Nevertheless, a common structure undergirds all of them: the human being is fundamentally related to something greater, whether formulated as nature itself, God, or some other suprapersonal entity, and that greater entity is connected with all other natural entities. This common structure was recognized during what Karl Jaspers referred to as the Axial Age, a period that dawned just before and just beyond the first millennium BCE, and an age in which philosophical, spiritual, and religious movements flourished across the world.

In ancient Greece, it began with the Ionian Enchantment, as coined by Harvard historian of science Gerald Holton, when Thales of Miletus, commonly recognized as the first philosopher of the Western world, attempted to explain the world scientifically without appealing to the Greek gods. It wasn't until Socrates, though, that *philosophia*, philosophy—the love of wisdom—caught fire. Plato's Academy, the first known university in the Western world, still memorialized in our word "academics," was an attempt to continue Socratic dialogue beyond the death of Socrates by serving as a formal institution dedicated to rational inquiry. In Plato's greatest student, Aristotle—who came to be known simply as *Ille Philosophus*, "the philosopher," in medieval times—philosophy became systematic. Having left the Academy when it was passed down to Plato's nephew,

Speusippus, Aristotle founded the Lyceum and espoused a teleological account of *phusis* (nature) that recognized the proper *telos* (end) of human beings to be *eudaimonia*, literally "good spirit," which he understood as "living well" by actively living out one's proper function as the *zoon logon echon*, that is, as the living being having *logos*, a rich word that in this context means a rational principle. Western metaphysics—inquiry that operates above and beyond *phusis*—was very much underway.

Raphael's *The School of Athens* provides an apt depiction of its initiation. In it, Plato is pointing upward, while Aristotle is gesturing downward. As it turns out, *phusis*, signified by Aristotle, and metaphysics, signified by Plato, are indeed both necessary and interrelated, which we need to understand if we are to recognize the proper place of human beings in nature.

In the East, a similar "awakening" occurred through the spiritual traditions of Daoism and Confucianism in China. Laozi, the supposed "author" of the *Daodejing* (*supposed* because Laozi literally simply means "old master," and it is very likely that the book is the result of an oral tradition that was finally written down rather than the thoughts of a single person), recognized an interdependent relationship between *dao* (the way of nature) and *de* (an individual's unique way of flourishing naturally). Kongzi, the great cultural leader of China more commonly known in the West by his Latinized name, Confucius, thought through the human relationship with *dao* at more of a social than natural level than the Daoists—but the social, of course, still operates in the realm of nature. Thus, the phrase "Confucian by day, Daoist by night" is a fitting one to encapsulate the cultivation of one's cultural and natural selves, both of which function in complementary ways to enable a person to achieve wholeness. In China, philosophy is not merely *philosophia*, the "love of wisdom," but *zhe xue*, the study of wisdom, a study that is meant to inform one's everyday existence and life's overall trajectory.

A similar story unfolds in India through their two main spiritual traditions, Hinduism and Buddhism. The Upanishads function as the primal texts guiding Hinduism. Like the *Daodejing*, they are the result of an oral tradition that was eventually written down. In them, the basic structure of reality is outlined as a relationship between *Atman*, the individual soul, and *Brahman*, the ultimate reality. In *moksha*, the Hindu word for enlightenment, one realizes that *Atman is Brahman* and *Brahman is Atman*—or, to put it in an inverse way using the words of Led Zeppelin, that "all is one and one is all." In the Advaita Vedanta sect that eventually springs from Hinduism, *moksha* entails the realization that *Brahman is Purusha*—that is, the cosmic self—in such a way that ultimate reality is synonymous with a supreme consciousness that is the source of all existence. The *Bhavagad Gita*, the primary influence for the work of Mahatma Gandhi, ultimately tells this very story in the form of an epic.

The same quest for discovering ultimate reality guided Siddhartha Gautama, now known by most as simply the Buddha, who saw humans as deeply connected with nature and thus did away with any belief in *Brahman* as *Purusha*. In *nirvana*, the Buddhist word for enlightenment that inspired the name of the grunge band, one realizes *sunyata*, that is, the emptiness of any independent self (known in Buddhism as *anatman*, literally "no-self") by recognizing the doctrine of *pratityasamutpada*, that is, the doctrine of "interdependent arising" in which one recognizes the interconnectedness of all natural entities. Although the various sects of Buddhism differ, especially regarding their understanding of the means to enlightenment, the doctrine of *pratityasamutpada* has been passed down to Tibet in Tenzin Gyatso, better known as His Holiness the 14th Dalai Lama, as well as to philosopher Keiji Nishitani in Japan.

Finally, the Axial Age proved pivotal to the great religious traditions. In Israel, the *navi* and *nevia*, the Hebrew name for prophets—literally, those who speak for God—had understood the divine as undeniably monotheistic, which is why the first commandment insists upon having no gods other than the one true God. Eventually, this monotheistic conception of God was merged with the Persian prophet Zarathustra's (known to the Greeks as Zoroaster) dual understanding of the cosmic struggle between Ahura Mazda, the God of light and truth, and Ahriman, the embodiment of darkness and evil. As it turned out, the combination of one true God and the cosmic struggle between light and dark—

that is, between good and evil—informed the big three religions of the West: Judaism, Christianity, and Islam.

Judaism recognizes two primary internal inclinations in humans, namely, the *yetzer ha tov* that is inclined toward good, and the *yetzer ha ra* that is inclined toward evil. Christianity takes up this narrative and applies it more broadly in a Zoroastrian framework as a cosmic battle between good and evil with the conception of God and Satan. In this tradition, Jesus of Nazareth, the anointed one (the Christ) eventually came to be understood as God incarnate in human form, that is, as the Holy Spirit embodied perfectly in the mode of a human being. In Islam, born from the night of revelations (the *Laylat al Qadr* sometimes referred to as "the Night of Power and Excellence") and the actions thereafter of Muhammad in Saudi Arabia, understood by Muslims as "the Seal of the prophets," we get a similar narrative of a struggle between good and evil with the right path ultimately lying in submission to Allah, their name for the one true God (the very word "Islam" means "submission" in Arabic, and Muslims are those who have submitted).

The overarching point is that humanity—naturally, and across all cultures, whether through philosophy, spirituality, or religion—has recognized an interconnection with the rest of nature but has formulated it in various ways. Nevertheless, the heart of the narrative stays the same because it is true: human flourishing happens in the context of embracing one's relation to nature—however and variously it can be understood—since humans *are* natural beings. Moreover, nature or God, or whatever one prefers to call the suprapersonal entity—the entity that transcends the individual human being—connects humans with the rest of creation. This connection has taken on various names but ultimately can be framed as a *field-focus model*. Individual entities are focal realities, but they are all interrelated in a field. Furthermore, the whole—the field—is greater than the sum of its parts—the foci—since the mediated relationships between the foci also form the field.

Recent developments in neuroscience and systems theory demonstrate the evolutionary progress of the human mind and its relationship with the rest of the natural world in ways that corroborate the great philosophical and spiritual traditions of the past—both West and East—that formed when humanity was more primal and more attuned (and subject) to nature. Moreover, the same structure of reality can be found in the big three Western religions, even if they have a decidedly supernatural bent. Jungian psychology informs us of the archetypes, that is, the primary structural elements of the human psyche that transcend and unite spiritual traditions—the yang and the yin of Daoism is the light and darkness of Zoroastrianism that informed the Western spiritual traditions of Judaism, Christianity, and Islam. The Hindu version of enlightenment as *moksha* and the Buddhist *nirvana* strike a similar chord to Western notions of enlightenment as expressed by Kant as *Aufklärung*—a "clearing up from under." In both the West and the East, we recognize enlightenment, that is, the awakening of consciousness to a more profound understanding of reality, as a lighting from the dark. Psychology can help us to see the connections between the Eastern and Western understandings of reality—and the human connection with nature in particular, which can then be corroborated with our findings in neuroscience in terms of our understanding of the human brain and systems theory in regard to how we are part of the broader system of nature.

In order to reunite humanity with nature—to breathe life into the rational animal—we need to connect the trajectory of nature with the trajectory of humanity, thus shedding light on the whole in relation to its creation, connecting the field and the focus, the *dao* and the *de*. The path is clear: We need to glimpse the nature of ultimate reality, known in the West as *phusis* or *natura*, and in the East as *tian* or *sunyata*. We then have to recognize the proper nature of the human being as intrinsically connected to nature. The Greek conception of *psuche* (what is called psyche or mind) as embodied rationality *and* animality requires elucidation. Next, we need to corroborate this primal conception with our current knowledge of the human brain and its evolutionary history. Anthony Stevens's work in evolutionary psychology will prove crucial. Finally, we must connect this scientific knowledge with systems theory, the *Gaia* of James Lovelock's hypothesis, to make humans whole and recognize our proper place in nature.

Throughout, we must recognize truth in Laozi's wisdom that "the *dao* that can be named is not the eternal *dao*" and Aristotle's dictum to look for precision just so far as the nature of the subject admits—and thus we must paint in broad strokes. Moreover, we must—at all times throughout this journey—recognize truth in the Zen koan "If you meet the Buddha on the road, kill him." We don't have time for false prophets and yet we have no choice but to be open to the mystery, knowing full well that we are merely human, all too human, and yet connected to something greater.

Let us begin.

CHAPTER 1
LOGOS DEPARTING FROM *DAO*

We begin, as we must begin, with the word. In ancient Greece, the word is denoted as *logos* and in ancient China as *dao*. Both *logos* and *dao* are polysemous, but we can glean a dual sense of these ideas. For Heraclitus, a philosopher who came after Thales but before Socrates, *logos* is the name for the underlying ordering principle of the universe *and* the name for the human ability to think, reason, and make sense of it through *dia-logos*, literally *through logos*—dialogue. In the first verse of the *Daodejing*, the most sacred text in Daoism, we learn that "the *dao* that can be named is not the eternal *dao*," where the word *dao* signifies the way of nature *and* the naming of the *dao*—that is, it functions as both a noun *and* a verb. The *Daodejing* comes to us with a warning that the ultimate reality cannot be known exhaustively. And yet, in the West at least since the Enlightenment, we have acted as if humans are superior to the way of nature and that we are thus the rightful masters over nature since we can glimpse its inner essence—that we have named the underlying ordering principle of nature. This hubris was formed over the course of Western history. We need to know this story to right the civilizational ship.

While Thales is the first philosopher in the West, and Socrates was the first well-known philosopher to live the philosophical life, the examined life worth living as he so famously put it, Aristotle was the first *systematic* philosopher. His writings span ethics, politics, psychology, rhetoric, biology (both botany *and* zoology), physics, and metaphysics, among other realms. Like his teacher Plato, he believed that philosophy begins in wonder (*thaumazein*) and that humans are naturally curious, a fact young parents soon find out when their toddlers continuously ask them "why." Plato believed that human beings are natural beings but needed *paideia*, that is, education or, better yet, *informed enculturation*, in order to see things as they really are and thus become enlightened. Ideally, this education happens early on, which is why the word *paideia* also refers to the upbringing of a child—our English word "pediatrics" was originally spelled "paediatrics," meaning doctor (*iatros*) of child (*pais*).

Plato utilizes the allegory of the cave to describe the process of *paideia* by imagining a group of prisoners who have been chained inside a dark cave their entire lives looking at the cave wall. Behind them is a fire where people hold up various objects between the fire and the wall, thus casting shadows on the wall. Since the shadows are all the prisoners have ever experienced, they believe that this is the ultimate reality and name and interpret the shadows as if they are real things even though they signify merely *doxes*, that is, mere beliefs as propagated by popular opinion. However, one of the prisoners breaks loose and makes his way out of the cave. At first, he is blinded by the sunlight, but as his eyes adjust and he sees things as they actually are—as illuminated by the sun, a metaphor for truth in this allegory—he becomes enlightened. When he goes back down to the cave to share his revelation with his fellow prisoners, they cannot understand him; they even mock him. In this allegory, Plato is attempting to show the difference between those who let others do thinking for them—that is, those who are not informed, the ones he calls *apaideusia* (meaning, roughly, uneducated)—and those who are informed of the ultimate truth, namely, the philosophers who had gone through the process of *paideia*. He is also warning that those who can see things as they are might have a difficult time in showing the truth to others.

Plato writes mainly in dialogue form, like a play, with Socrates usually serving as the main character in his works; thus, any claims of Plato's true philosophical doctrine should be met with suspicion. Indeed, he may very well have preferred the form of dialogue in order to show us the processual nature of philosophical thinking—the unfolding of *dia-logos*—so that we can learn to think for ourselves rather than to attempt to convince us of the Truth, the whole Truth, and nothing but the Truth. Nevertheless, in piecing together Plato's thought and attempting to attribute some coherence to it, we come to see that he seemed to believe that the true world is not what it appears to be in our everyday interactions with it. *Phusis*, the Greek word for nature that encompasses the *phys*ical realm (the Greek upsilon "u" typically gets translated as a "y" in English) is *informed* by *eidos* or *idea*, which has come to be known as Plato's notion of the Form. In Greek, *eidos* is the name for the outward look or "form" of an entity. *Idea* also means "form" in Greek, but it is more a matter of *idea*tion in Plato's framework in that it refers to a universal, intellectual blueprint that is *abstracted from* (literally "pulled away" from) but *related to* things as they appear in *phusis* (nature). In achieving enlightenment, Plato believed that a person was able to see the universal true Forms, the intellectual blueprints or templates of things, rather than merely see the ever-fleeting and perishable concrete entities as they appear. In the context of the famous allegory, the enlightened one can see the light through the shadows. Plato pointing upward in *The School of Athens* is Raphael's way of noting that the true reality for Plato is something higher than everyday experience.

Aristotle, depicted next to Plato in Raphael's fresco, is gesturing downward to signify Aristotle's understanding of "the form" to be inherent in the things themselves, as opposed to situating it in some higher plane of reality as Plato did. While Aristotle respected Plato, he once noted that truth is more important than friendship, even if both should be honored. Thus, rather than maintaining allegiance to Plato's philosophy, Aristotle's thought moved in a different direction that was closer to nature. Aristotle's father, Nicomachus, was a physician whose interest in the natural world and medicine seems to have deeply influenced Aristotle's approach. While Nicomachus the *physician* attempted to heal the body in relation to *phusis*, Aristotle the philosopher attempted to gain wisdom as to the proper human place in nature more broadly. In doing so, he often appealed to examples in medicine to make his points. He sometimes referred to Presocratic philosophers like Thales or Heraclitus as *phusikoi*—that is, as physicists—since they were seeking the truth about *phusis*, a trait that Aristotle shared. Our word "naturalist," as applied to Henry David Thoreau, John Muir, or Aldo Leopold, for instance, functions in a similar fashion.

For our purposes, what is most important is Aristotle's understanding of the human relationship with *phusis*. He understood all living beings (*bios*, which is where we get our word "biology") to have *psuche*, which we typically translate as "mind," "soul," or "spirit" but probably meant something like "that which breathes life into being." Our word "psychology" is derived from the Greek root *psuche*. Instead of looking to Platonic Forms for the form or "true nature" of a living being, Aristotle situated it in the being itself. The naturalist in him separated out different types of *psuche*: plants have different guiding principles (*logoi*) than animals (*zoa*, which is where we get our name "zoo"). For Aristotle, the human being is the *zoon logon echon*, the animal having *logos*. While other living beings have principles that guide their unique development in this account, only the human being has the power to articulate these principles—and thus we are the "rational animal," even if, as we will see, the Latin *ratio* doesn't quite mean the same thing as *logos* as the concept unfolds in Western history. We can study *bios* (living things) and make an account of our findings, thus creating a biology; we can be more specific in studying *zoa* (animals), thus constricting our lens to a zoology. Filled with wonder (*thaumazein*), Aristotle seemed to want to study it all and thus became a *polymath* (meaning learned in many things).

Regardless of the focus of our lens, when it comes to living things, Aristotle believed that they all are striving toward *telos*, which we can understand as their proper or *natural* end. The *telos* is the end, and the *logos* is the means to get there that can be explained rationally using human language (the other sense of the word *logos*). Thus, someone versed in botany could come up with an account (*logos*), so to speak, of the conditions needed for an acorn to reach its proper end as a flourishing oak tree. Since humans are natural beings, we too have a proper end, which Aristotle understood as *eudaimonia*, which literally means "good spirit." *Daimon* is the word the Greeks used for a guiding force that transcended the individual itself, while *psuche* is the more generic term for that which breathes life into being, even if they both get translated sometimes as "spirit." Socrates famously spoke of his *daimonion*, by which he meant "a divine something" that would guide him.

In Aristotle's framework, this *eudaimonia*—understood as the good life—consists in actively living in accordance with *arete* in order to achieve one's proper end (*telos*). The word *arete* is typically translated as virtue and means an excellent trait of the self that helps one achieve one's proper end. Aristotle lists several ethical virtues throughout his works, such as patience, truthfulness, and courage, as well as intellectual virtues that lead to good reasoning and understanding. The person who achieves *eudaimonia* is a person who has cultivated the virtues through practice to such an extent that he or she can do the right thing at the right time in the right context consistently. Importantly, the *eu* (the good) in *eudaimonia* had both prescriptive and descriptive functions: living well entails living in accordance with one's proper nature as connected with the natural world in general. A deviation from one's proper end through repeatedly practicing *kakies* (vices) can pervert one's path to goodness and leave one with a bad *ethos* (character).

While Aristotle insists that humans are the *rational* animal, he also explores how desire (*orexis*) plays a role in the individual striving toward one's proper end. He differentiated between desire for bodily pleasure (*epithumia*), spirited desire (*thumos*), and rational desire (*boulesis*), all of which exist in the human *psuche* or psyche. Virtue (*arete*) is not merely about right reason for Aristotle, but also about having the right desires. Ultimately, one balances reason (*logos*) and desire (*orexis*) to achieve one's proper (natural) end (*telos*). A sex addict has an improper balance of reason and desire regarding one's perceived need for sex and pleasure (*epithumia*), thus enabling this craving to warp one's character (*ethos*). Similarly, a person who has a bad temper and easily flies off the handle in anger has an improper balance of reason and desire regarding *thumos*. Ideally, the human being develops a rational desire (*boulesis*) to achieve *eudaimonia* and has the tools to deliberate, using *logos* to achieve one's proper end.

In the West, Aristotle was the first thinker to put together a systematic logic, a logic of *logos*, so to speak. In doing so, he allowed for the possibility of *logos* as named to supersede *logos* as the underlying ordering principle of nature. Eventually, *logos* became Latinized as *ratio*. Stoic philosophers like Marcus Aurelius and Seneca the Younger recognized *ratio* (reason) as a powerful tool for understanding the natural order of the universe. Indeed, following reason was the path to virtue (*virtus*) and to achieving one's proper end (*finis*), thus achieving the highest good (*summum bonum*) in a similar way as seen in Aristotle: *eudaimonia* (living well—or, more literally, "good spirit") meant living in accordance with *arete* (virtue) in order to achieve one's proper *telos* (end). The Stoics agreed that human flourishing meant aligning one's life with nature, which they understood as *natura*. There seemed to arise, however, something very *unnatural* in the Stoic understanding of balancing reason and emotions. As Stoicism evolves, the concept of *ataraxia*, that is, mental tranquility, comes to take on increasing importance. This term refers to a state of freedom from emotional disturbance, and Stoics would practice *meditatio*, that is, meditations—understood as ritualized reflections— to maintain it. In the *Encheiridion*, Epictetus reminds us that, in the act of kissing one's child, we should remember the child will one day die just as one's favorite bowl could one day break, thus preparing oneself mentally for the loss of a child, should such a misfortune befall oneself. While the overarching goal of retaining one's mental tranquility by only focusing on what one can control (one's response to such a possible disaster in this context) and not on what one cannot control (in this case, the possible death of one's child), one can see how a life in which a person repeatedly adopts a Stoic approach may lend oneself to desensitization. It is natural, of course, for a parent to mourn the loss of a child to an untimely death, as any parent who has lost one knows at a visceral level. Yet while Stoicism is ultimately Aristotelian in that the goal is to strive toward balancing reason and desire or emotion, an infatuation with *ataraxia* might sew the seed of reason overcoming—rather than complementing—desire or emotion. In the end, what we really need is a balance between reason and desires and emotions.

In order to tell the story of the elevation of *ratio* over *anima* in the Western world, of reason over spirit—concepts known to the Greeks as *logos* and *psuche*, respectively—we need to adjust our lens toward religion, which featured another pivotal development in the Axial Age. As the Roman Empire expanded, the decidedly Greek influence of *logos* being the rational guiding principle of nature that came to be known as *ratio* was met with Judaism's understanding of the highest good as a *super*natural single being. Early Judaism recognized Elohim as the various gods of the world, but eventually, through the prophecy of Moses, the one true God was revealed as Yahweh, a name first revealed to Abraham centuries before Moses. The first decree in the covenant between humanity and God, as revealed to Moses from Yahweh, is to respect Yahweh as the one true God, as directed by the first commandment, and the second is to do away with idolatry—that is, the worship of anything other than God. The Jewish God as revealed in the *Tanakh*—consisting of the five books of Moses (the *Torah*), the *Nevi'im* (the words of the prophets), and the related sacred writings (the *Ketuvim*), core texts that also compose the Old Testament of the Christian Bible—reveal God as a force of both good and evil. Obedience to God is met with *hesed* (loving-kindness) in Judaism, as it places humanity in God's good graces, while disobedience to God is met with *zaham* (anger or wrath), leading to punishment in the form of plagues, natural disasters, and destruction.

Various passages in the *Tanakh*, or the Old Testament, speak of the coming of a *mashiach*, a messiah or anointed one (the Greek word for this is *xristos*, Christ) descending from King David who will usher in an era of *shalom* (peace) and initiate a harmonious relationship with humanity and God. Eventually, Jesus of Nazareth came to be seen as this person. The Roman emperor Constantine came to believe this, leading to the Christianization of the Roman Empire. Early debates about the nature of Jesus revolved around whether he was a prophet (one who speaks for God) or actually God in the form of a human. Eventually, through various councils (gatherings of Christian leaders), in this case the Councils of Nicaea, Ephesus, and Chalcedon, it was decided that Jesus was, in fact, God incarnate. The Christian God is thus understood as a trinity—a combination of three in one all at the same time—in God the Father, Son, and Holy Spirit, with the latter known in Latin as the *Spiritus Sanctus*. God the Father is the transcendent creator and God the Son is Jesus Christ, the anointed one who was informed by the Holy Spirit, which is the Christian notion of the active presence of God in the world.

The Roman Empire provides a key transition in our understanding of the human-nature relationship. The first Roman emperor, Gaius Julius Caesar Augustus, considered himself a god in human form among the other Roman gods, which reflected the gods of ancient Greece via the *Interpretatio Romana*, the Roman interpretation of Greek deities (e.g., Jupiter aligning with Zeus, Venus with Aphrodite, Baccus with Dionysus, etc.). Years later, Marcus Aurelius ascended to emperor, initiating a Stoic understanding of *ratio* as guiding human beings to align with *natura*, nature. Even later, the Roman emperor Constantine adopted a Christian approach in which humans were understood to be *imago Dei*, that is, made in the image or likeness of God, with Jesus Christ's life as God incarnate—literally, God in the form of flesh—serving as the guide for persons wishing to live in the grace of God. The first four books of the New Testament of the Christian Bible, the Gospels (the *God-spel*, the story of God), known in Greek as the *euangelion* (the "good news," which is where we get our word "evangelical"), chronicle the life of Jesus as recounted by Matthew, Mark, Luke, and John, two of whom served as part of the twelve disciples in Jesus's carnal life. In Matthew, Jesus is revealed as "the king of the Jews," thus fulfilling Old Testament prophecies. In Mark, Jesus is hailed as the Son of God. In Luke, Jesus is presented as a savior of the marginalized members of society, thus calling him "the Son of Man." Finally, in John, Jesus is called the *word* of God, that is, the divine *logos*. This is sometimes translated by Christian thinkers as the "incarnate word." Paul, who popularized early Christianity, describes Jesus as "the image of the invisible God, the firstborn of all creation" in Colossians 1:15, a crucial verse of the Bible for any Christian to understand. In this verse, Paul attempted to show that Jesus was indeed God in human form—and thus any person who wanted to live a life of grace, a Christian life, had better pay close attention to the stories we have of Jesus Christ.

Early medieval philosophers had to grapple with the towering influences of Plato and Aristotle of ancient Greece *and* the Christian notion of the trinitarian nature of reality—that is, true reality being understood as God the Father, the Son, and the Holy Spirit, with humans now understanding their place in the *Scala Naturae*, "the scale of nature," in a hierarchical fashion, fixed somewhere between God and the lower animals. While made in the image of God (*imago Dei*), humans were still understood to be the *animal rationale* in Augustine's account, the first of the great medieval philosophers who was eventually canonized as a saint. Augustine came to understand humanity as having an earthly—that is, animal—existence, but he also maintained that humans are capable of living in "the city of God," a spiritual community (literally "with unity") in which souls are unified by their love of God. *Anima*, the Latin word for *psuche*, loses priority to the *Spiritus Sanctus*, initiating the rift that will ultimately tear apart the rational animal in the West. *Spiritus* still carries the notion of breath with it, as echoed in our word "re*spir*ation," but it has more of a divine ring to it than *anima*, by which we get our words for "animation" and "animal." Augustine's dualistic framework—spirit versus animal—provided the possibility for medieval persons to ascribe to *contemptus mundi*, a contempt for the material world in which humans set their ultimate sights on spiritual salvation and come to hate the world in the material sense. Nearly a millennium after Augustine, through his teacher Albertus Magnus, who grappled with the commentaries of ancient Greek philosophy by the great Muslim philosophers Ibn Sina (Latinized as Avicenna) and Ibn Rushd (Latinized as Averroes), the philosopher Aquinas understood *contemptus mundi* to be a means to pursue *virtu* (virtue) and achieve *beatitudo*, his term for the highest form of happiness, which could only be achieved through a supernatural union with God in the afterlife.

Although Aquinas is commonly regarded as the person who best synthesized Aristotelianism with Christian theology, situating the highest good, the *summum bonum*, as *beatitudo* in a supernatural pursuit has a very different flavor from *eudaimonia* as achieving one's natural end in Aristotle, even if the *daimon* in ancient Greece had suprapersonal connotations. There is nothing in Aristotle's corpus that suggests anything like a contempt of the material world. The concept of *contemptus mundi* did not flourish in an Islamic context since the prophet Muhammad emphasized the importance of enjoying permissible pleasures as long as they are *Inshallah*—that is, as long as they align with the will of Allah, their word for the one true God. Both Ibn Sina and Ibn Rushd followed Aristotle in seeking balance and moderation to achieve the good life, while aligning their philosophy with elements of Islam. Aquinas, canonized as a saint in 1323 CE, aligned the Roman Catholic Church more with *contemptus mundi* than its Middle Eastern counterpart in Islam.

Given the towering influence of Aristotle across cultures, the American educator Max Lerner rightly notes that "no single thinker, not even Plato, has had as much impact as Aristotle on the intellectual and institutional history of later centuries." Allegiance to Aristotle was a must during medieval times in the West, even if that allegiance looked different in different cultural contexts. It wasn't until Francis Bacon and René Descartes, during the dawn of the Enlightenment period, that the West engaged in a full-on assault of Aristotelianism. Blind allegiance to *Ille Philosophus*, the philosopher, became understood as a form of idolatry. On the heels of the bubonic plague, "the Black Death" as it was called, that spread across and around Europe, Bacon swapped out the medieval *Scala Naturae* for his own understanding of the natural world that was guided by an inductive method in which specific observations of nature are meant to guide more general principles, with the culmination meant to unveil nature's underlying structure. This emphasis on induction was coupled with Descartes's "rules for the direction of the mind," which emphasized gaining clarity and distinctness of an idea, then reducing its complexity to its simplest terms and procedurally and systematically arranging it back together in an orderly fashion to attain exhaustive truth. Anyone who has taken apart and put back together a complex machine is familiar with this way of thinking.

Cartesian reasoning (reasoning that aligns with the method of Descartes), "*rational*ism" as it would be eventually called, led to the conclusion that mind and matter are essentially different substances. His famous dictum *cogito ergo sum*—"I think, therefore, I am"—emphasized that the rightful identity of the human being resides in the mind, in an "unextended," that is, immaterial, substance. Moreover, he argued that all matter is essentially the same and differs only in terms of its arrangements. No longer should we seek to understand the proper natural end, the *telos*, of any natural entity, as was done in Aristotelian science. Instead, we should set our sights on mapping out the ways in which the entirety of matter operates uniformly in space and time, a task bequeathed to Isaac Newton.

Using Cartesian coordinates, Newton was the first to invent—in the original Latin sense of to discover—the calculus, which he believed was an unveiling of the mathematical reasoning of God. Through it, he was able to develop the three laws of motion that he believed governed over the entirety of matter. If Ockam's razor is true—that the simplest explanation is indeed best—Newton seemed to land upon the truth about reality: all matter, regardless of type, functions in the same way in that (1) an object at rest will stay at rest and an object in motion will stay in motion until an external force diverts it; (2) the force of something can be calculated by multiplying its mass and acceleration; and (3) for every action, there is an equal and opposite reaction. Anyone who has played a game of billiards can appreciate the beauty of Newton's discovery: the pool balls are all the same shape and hold the same weight, so on a level surface a master pool player can get really good at anticipating where the balls will fall, given their original arrangement and the force with which the cue ball is struck at a given angle.

Curiously enough, though, Gottfried Wilhelm Leibniz discovered the calculus at roughly the same time as Newton but came upon a very different conclusion as to the nature of matter. Rather than thinking that all matter is identical and can be understood exhaustively using simple laws, he attempted to hold on to the Aristotelian notion of *telos* by positing the existence of "monads," which are simple, indivisible substances that perceive the universe in their own unique way and exist together in a preestablished harmony as designed by the cosmic choreographer, God. Thus from a Leibnizian perspective, Newton's physics may be able to predict where a pool ball will land, but it cannot adequately explain how the sunflower "knows" how to follow the sun. For Leibniz, matter is "spirited" in that it can perceive the world around it and has *telos* built into it such that it "knows" how to follow nature's innate principles in order to flourish. Through his interactions with Jesuit missionaries who had been to China, Leibniz was exposed to Chinese thought, and while it is unclear that his system of monads was influenced by it in the way that his understanding of binary coding (the 0s and 1s that compose modern computing) was informed by the *I Ching* (the ancient Chinese manual of divination), the universe he posits sounds eerily familiar to the focus-field models that informed Neo-Confucianism, the dominant philosophical school during his time in China, which blended aspects of Daoism and Confucianism with Buddhist ideas that came from India. The difference is that Leibniz needed to posit the existence of God to account for the interactions between things, as he considered monads to be "windowless," while Eastern models tend to situate the ultimate symphony of creation and destruction in nature itself. Even if our current annotation of the calculus follows Leibniz rather than Newton, Newtonian physics ultimately won the day and the idea of matter in a state of perceptively striving toward an end (matter as in-*telos*, or entelechy), was, for the most part, abandoned.

Descartes's *rationalism* and Bacon's *empiricism* became the standing party line of Enlightenment thinkers. Christian Wolff was the intellectual heir of Leibniz and argued vigorously for deductive, rational thinking as the means to discover truth, while David Hume thought through the logical consequences of Newton's empiricism and ultimately came upon Hume's guillotine: the claim that one cannot infer prescriptive or normative claims from descriptive ones. The leap from *is* to *ought*, from how things *are* to how things *should be*, in Hume's account, cannot be bridged using reason, highlighting a fundamental departure from Aristotle's understanding of the good (*eu*) of a living being aligning with its natural unfolding toward its end (*telos*). It wasn't until Immanuel Kant, who initially followed in the dogmatic tradition of Leibniz and Wolff but was eventually awoken from his dogmatic slumber by Hume, that rationalism and empiricism came together. In Kant's so-called "Copernican revolution," he supposed that objects must conform to our knowledge, rather than the other way around, in an inversion similar to the way in which Copernicus understood the sun, not the earth, as the center of the universe. Ultimately, Kant believed that *phenomena*, appearances, are what humans experience, as organized by our senses (empirically) and our mind (rationally), while *noumena*, the "things in themselves," cannot be known as they are in themselves.

German philosopher Georg Wilhelm Friedrich Hegel's *Phenomenology of Spirit* goes beyond Kant by attempting to bridge the knowable and the noumenal. In it, Hegel shows us how ideas progress in his dialectic (meaning *through lo-*

gos) from a thesis (that which is initially posited) to an antithesis (that which opposes it), and finally to a synthesis (that which combines aspects of each). Through the process of self-consciousness he outlines, one eventually realizes the *Absoluter Geist*, the Absolute Spirit, which is his word for the ultimate reality in which a person (1) understands oneself, (2) understands nature, and (3) sees how everything is connected. This process of self-development, called *Bildung* by Hegel, mirrors what the Greeks understood as *paideia*. Hegel's friend Friedrich Hölderlin poeticized the relationship between *Sterbliche* (mortals) and *das Heilige* (the holy), a concept that would influence Martin Heidegger in his later understanding of *Dasein* (human existence) and *Sein* (being).

Hegel's onetime roommate, Friedrich Wilhelm Joseph Schelling, believed that humans are nature rendered in conscious form and thus argued that the same rational principles that operate in human consciousness also operate in nature. He also posited the existence of a pre-logical "dark fire" or "blind desire" at work in the *Geist*, a concept that would eventually inform an understanding of the unconscious. Arthur Schopenhauer's concept of the will to live (*der Wille zum Leben*) explores the unconscious as a blind, aimless striving that makes up the underlying force of reality. For him, there is no *telos* involved and thus life is inherently suffering without any rhyme or reason. Eduard von Hartmann, on the other hand, saw the unconscious as the ultimate ground of reality, noting that it is made up of *two* features: will and reason. Combining Darwinian science and Hegelian philosophy, he argued for a teleological account in which humans are animals that had evolved enough to become conscious but were still ultimately bound to the unconscious.

Hartmann became an object of ridicule for Friedrich Nietzsche in his *Untimely Meditations*, where he calls him a "hotch-potch philosopher," and Hartmann's notion of the unconscious in particular became the target Franz Brentano's *Psychology from an Empirical Standpoint*, in which Brentano calls Hartmann's unconscious "something purely imaginary" and intentionally argued that the goal of psychology should be to establish exact laws. Interestingly, his student, Sigmund Freud, would go on to found the discipline of psychology—in which the unconscious would come to be seen as playing a pivotal role in influencing human behavior. Edmund Husserl, who studied directly under Brentano ten years after Freud, would found phenomenology, adopting the motto "back to the things themselves," which for him meant interpreting the world as it appears rather than engaging in the lofty intellectual pursuits that had become commonplace in German idealism from the likes of Hegel, Schelling, and others. Husserl vowed to remain true to consciousness, while Freud ventured into the labyrinth of the unconscious.

Psychology and phenomenology seemed destined to drift apart since Carl Jung and Martin Heidegger, the respective students of Freud and Husserl, never met. Heidegger traveled to Zurich, Switzerland, Jung's home base, in 1936 to deliver a lecture on art, and then again in 1959 to share his philosophical insights to the psychological community there via Medard Boss, as he was convinced that his philosophy could benefit people, especially those in need of help. Jung, who lived just down the road, was busy working through his own theory of the collective unconscious in 1936 (influenced heavily, as it turns out, by Hartmann) and thus did not attend Heidegger's lecture. The elderly Jung was also absent in 1959, even though he and Boss were close colleagues, as he was working through *Man and His Sym-*

bols, the work that will prove essential in joining philosophy with psychology in the next chapter. While both Ludwig Binswanger, who introduced Heidegger's thought to Boss, and Boss himself attempted to bridge elements of thought from Heidegger and Jung, it is safe to say that, for the most part, philosophy and psychology as influenced by these two twentieth-century giants went their own directions. The joining of the two—of *logos* with *psuche*, the *ratio* with the *anima*—is the first step in healing the human relationship with nature.

CHAPTER 2
RECONNECTING *PSUCHE* WITH *PHUSIS*

Both Heidegger and Jung are penetrating thinkers whose oeuvres span volumes upon volumes of content, some of which is highly esoteric and thus difficult to follow. Luckily, though, both provided outlines of their thinking to a more general audience at various stages throughout their careers. Heidegger would periodically provide public lectures and Jung, just before his death, agreed to publish *Man and His Symbols*, a collaboration with his closest colleagues that provides a high-level overview of Jungian psychology written in English. Bringing the two together can help to initiate the first of two Gestalt shifts regarding the human relationship to nature, the initial paradigm shift serving as a means to decenter the human subject as merely rational by connecting conscious life with the unconscious, thus viewing the human as a whole and breathing life into the rational animal. This initial shift will then provide the ground to leap toward the second shift and see the bigger picture of how the rational animal is intrinsically tied to nature—and indeed to the entirety of its creation.

Heidegger's magnum opus is *Being and Time*, which itself leads readers to a Gestalt shift in terms of providing a new understanding of the nature of what it means to be human. Heidegger begins the book with a quote from Plato's *Sophist*, in which Plato's dialogue questions whether we still understand the word "being." Heidegger responds to Plato by stating frankly that we no longer understand what it means *to be* an entity and sets out to raise anew "the question of being," the *Seinsfrage*, as he calls it. As he progresses through the book, we come to understand that the human being in the modern era (which began roughly around the time of Bacon and Descartes in the Enlightenment) came to be seen as a subject opposed to objects. The word "subject" literally means "thrown under" in Latin and is the translation for *hupokeimenon* in Greek, which means "that which lies beneath," meaning the source or ground of being. For the Greeks, the source of being was connected to *phusis* (nature), while in medieval times after the Roman Empire became Christianized, the human was understood to be *subjectum* to God, that is, a subject subordinate to ("ranked under") God the Creator in the *Scala Naturae*. As the modern period unfolded, the concept of the subject was turned on its head when the human individual came to understand oneself as the source of being, captured nearly perfectly in Descartes's famous phrase *cogito ergo sum*—"I think, therefore, I am." In Heidegger's interpretation, grounding humans as the source of being is akin to making the human being the measure of all things, a view held by the sophist Protagoras in ancient Greece. Much of Heidegger's thought is an attempt to show that this view is mere sophistry—that is, perhaps plausible at a superficial level but ultimately untrue. Sophistry is essentially untruth disguised as *sophia* (wisdom). Our word "sophomore" attempts to capture the fact that second-year students are in need of more wisdom.

In his *Principles of Philosophy*, Descartes calls *cogito ergo sum* the most certain proposition that one can possibly come upon using his rational method; in *Meditations on First Philosophy*, the *cogito* functions as Descartes's assurance that he exists as long as he is thinking. One of Heidegger's ultimate aims in *Being and Time* is to leave aside the abstract Cartesian reasoning that typified some discourse in the modern period and get "back to the things themselves," meaning to describe the world as it is actually experienced. In doing so, he moves away from talking about subjects and objects as primary and instead utilizes the term "Dasein" to refer to the existence of the human being. In this sense, he stays true to Husserl but also moves beyond him in that his understanding of Dasein—which, for our purposes, simply means "human existence"—does not align with Husserl's notion of consciousness. The word *Dasein* in German simply means "being-there" and, for Heidegger, Dasein is made up of built-in ontological structures—that is, ways of being that structure our existence, one of which is *In-der-Welt-Sein,* or "being-in-the-world." Heidegger is attempting to shift the way in which we understand the human relationship with reality by urging us that we are "always already," as he regularly puts it, in the world and do not primarily experience the world as a subject opposed to objects, even if that way of approaching reality is helpful in attempting to gain objective knowledge about the world (that is, in gaining knowledge that can be measured). Although a scientist can gain calculated and measurable data under controlled circumstances, Heidegger tries to show that our everyday engagement with the world is more akin to the carpenter who masterfully hammers a nail as we navigate life's everyday routines.

While Heidegger was attempting to describe the way in which entities show up while we are practically engaging with them, the predominance of the Cartesian way of understanding the human relationship to the world left him with language unsuitable to his project. Thus, he had to form his own language in the form of neologisms and connect concepts from the past (via Greek and Latin) to make his case. As a result, a foray into learning even the vocabulary of *Being and Time*, much less the structure of Heidegger's argument, is a significant task in and of itself. Luckily, Heidegger provided some public lectures to help explain his philosophy in lay terms. In them, he explains how Cartesian subjectivity combined with Newtonian physics initiated the possibility that an object comes *to be* only insofar as it stands opposed to a subject. This initiates, as he calls it, "The Age of the World Picture": an age in which everything, if considered to exist at all, must be defined in terms of calculable spatiotemporal magnitudes of uniform matter in motion. Our ability to represent the world in its entirety as a picture is a means to gain mastery over it, thus catapulting human beings as masters of the universe in quite a literal sense (with the uni-verse meaning an entity turned into one). Initially the world as pictured is confronted as *das Gegenständige*, that is, as objects *standing against* the subject in the modern period. But eventually, as we gain mastery over the world, the world begins to show up as *Bestand*, that is, as a repository of mere resources to be maximally exploited. We come to see the world as material on hand to be manipulated rationally and forget that all living entities are en-spirited. This forms the heart of the fissure in the human relationship with nature that we must repair.

It is because of this very narrative of the relationship between human beings and nature as one of master versus slave that we have come upon the crises we face as a human species: anthropogenic climate change is a result of humans exploiting nature's nonrenewable resources as if they were infinite; the Sixth Extinction is a result of us not recognizing our inherent relationship with other living beings as aspects of nature. For Heidegger, in the age of the world picture, we have catapulted ourselves as superior to everything nonhuman and, in doing so, have put ourselves into a precarious situation, since we are still dependent upon natural processes in order to flourish.

The means by which we frame reality in this way, to continue Heidegger's analogy of the world picture, leads to a new understanding of what it means *to be* in our contemporary era. Heidegger called this new human way of framing *Gestell*—with *stellen* meaning "to put" or "to place," and *Ge-* meaning to gather together, in this case in the sense of a totality. We can see the frame of *Gestell* at work in hydraulic fracturing technologies that attempt to extract the maximum amount of oil and gas from the ground by the most efficient and productive means, and also in geoengineering technologies that attempt to direct the planet's ecosystems to a more sustainable state as a response to the climate change–related effects of this very process of the extraction of oil and gas. Heidegger begins to see the lens of *Gestell* applied to humanity itself in the practice of human resources departments that attempt to extract as much labor from humans as possible, with productivity and efficiency serving as the ultimate guides. Anyone who works in a modern industrial setting has felt the frame of *Gestell*, even if one's work environment hasn't been framed in terms of Heidegger's language. Indeed, even realms that purportedly are driven by the care or cultivation of human beings—for instance, healthcare or education—are deeply informed by the frame of *Gestell*, as coupled with our current capitalistic framework, when the focus is on optimizing resource management (including *human* resources) and streamlining processes to align with maximum efficiency and productivity. Any patient or student who has experienced themselves as merely a number in a giant healthcare system or university has felt the frame of *Gestell*.

Much of Heidegger's later work is dedicated to thinking through a different understanding of what it means to be—and particularly what a different understanding of the human-nature relationship could look like. His so-called second magnum opus, *Contributions to Philosophy*, is filled with abstruse language but its ultimate aim is to knock humans off our collective pedestals as masters of the universe and initiate what he calls *Sachlichkeit*, a devotion to the *Sachen*, the things themselves as revealed by being. He believed that poets were the messengers of being and viewed the monumental German poet Hölderlin, in particular, to have glimpsed the fundamental nature of existence. Hölderlin's poem "As When on a Holiday" held special significance for Heidegger. Although it was written in 1800, it wasn't published until 1910. Heidegger interprets it to be a fitting reflection on the relationship between the human being and nature, and on the interconnections between the entirety of nature's creation.

In the poem, Hölderlin poeticizes about *aether*, his name for the father of light, and abyss, a reference to the dark, creative power of mother earth. Reality, for Hölderlin, is informed by spirit, and nature as spirit *inspires* (or *en-spirits*) every living thing, breathing life into her creation. Thus, everything is connected to nature and operates "according to established law" ("Nach festem Gesetz") as Hölderlin puts it, meaning humanity *is* according to the way in which nature remains present within it. This established law cannot be known exhaustively by humans, so Heidegger recommends *Verhaltenheit*, that is, restraint, in attempting to represent nature in exhaustive terms, as he goes through *Contributions to Philosophy*. For Heidegger, we must remain open to the mystery of nature's ever-dynamic unfolding.

What Heidegger is ultimately trying to do is to open us up to ways of understanding the human place in the natural world that do not fall prey to the myopic frame of *Gestell*.

Although *Contributions to Philosophy* is a difficult text that was only shown to a few of Heidegger's friends during his lifetime (it was not prepared for publication until after his death), he thankfully provides an outline for the type of thinking needed to initiate a change in the human-nature relationship in language prepared for a public audience, during a 1955 memorial address to celebrate the 175th birthday of the composer Conradin Kreutzer, in his hometown of Messkirch. In that address, he states that the frame of *Gestell* is circumscribed entirely by *rechnendes Denken*, calculative thinking that focuses on efficiency, practicality, and the manipulation of nature to align with human interests through rationally based, data-driven means. Calculative thinking is powerful and had resulted in astonishing advancements in mobile communication in Heidegger's day, which has only accelerated with the onset of "smart" phones, increasingly precise data analysis techniques and technologies to inform decisions, as well as—with the onset of generative artificial "intelligence"—increasingly sophisticated means to represent and manipulate entities in three-dimensional printing technologies and gene editing. The successes of calculative thinking are undeniable, a fact that Heidegger understood even if he preferred to spend much of his time at his rural hut in the Black Forest.

However, Heidegger warns in his address that it is increasingly becoming the *only* way of thinking that people find important. There is, he argues, another sort of thinking that belongs to the nature of humans, called *besinnliches Denken*, translated sometimes as "meditative," "contemplative," or "reflective" thinking. Meditative thinking might be the best translation in English due to its connection to mediation, as this sort of thinking is a thinking that mediates between the human and something beyond it. Contemplative thinking is probably too Platonic, in that it assumes the notion of a form, that is, a *template* or blueprint, that one is aligning with in one's thinking. However we choose to translate it, Heidegger warns in 1955 already that too many of us engage in thoughtlessness (*Bessinungslosigkeit*) as we spend our time distractedly chained to radio and television. The prevalence of calculative thinking and the lack of meditative thinking, the kind of thoughtlessness that is now embedded in social media algorithms that drive user feeds with the intent of diverting human attention toward it, takes away from our ability to think for ourselves.

Heidegger's notion of *besinnliches Denken* is a way to think for oneself, and to think about one's own existence in light of the whole of reality. The verb *besinnen* is a combination of *be*, which means "to" or "with," and *sinnen*, which means to think, consider, or be mindful—that is, to sense (*sinn*) with one's mind or spirit. Put together, meditative thinking is a reflective practice in which one thinks for oneself about how the parts are related to the whole— in this context, how the human being is related to nature more broadly. Heidegger ends the address quoting the poet Johann Peter Hebel, who argued that we are no different from plants, whether we like to admit it to ourselves or not, as we must rise from the earth in order to bloom into the aether and to bear fruit, with the earth symbolizing darkness and the aether symbolizing light, language that echoes Hölderlin. In another public-facing lecture that was delivered in Freiburg and later in Zurich, titled "The Origin of the Work of Art," Heidegger utilized the language of *Erde* (earth) and *Welt* (world) to function in the same way as earth and aether, respectively, ending that work with the words of Hölderlin himself. Putting the 1955 memorial address alongside Heidegger's public comments on Hölderlin, we can piece together that Heidegger clearly believed it was natural for us not merely to engage in rational thinking, but also to think deeply about our own natural way of unfolding in light of our being as an instantiation of nature.

Looking holistically at Heidegger's life and work, we know he saw resonance in his notion of *besinnliches Denken* not only in the German poetry of Hölderlin and Hebel, but also in the traditions of Daoism and Buddhism, and even in marginalized elements of the Christian tradition through Meister Eckhart. It seems, though, that Heidegger didn't explore the entire scope of the means by which meditative thinking occurs, at least in his published works. *Besinnung* is the word for reflection or contemplation in German, but it is also a word for consciousness. The word *besinnungslos* as an adjective means "senseless" or "unconscious," a topic that didn't receive much of Heidegger's attention. Although he used the term *Bessinungslosigkeit* in his memorial address in 1955, he clearly meant "senselessness" or "thoughtlessness"; he wasn't referring explicitly to the unconscious in a psychological sense in that context.

However, the terrain of the unconscious is dealt with briefly by Heidegger in his commentary on Freud in the Zollikon Seminars in Zurich. For Freud, the unconscious is a reservoir of desires, feelings, and even thoughts that exists outside of our conscious awareness but nevertheless influences human behavior. In the context of the seminar, Medard Boss asks Heidegger how he would examine the case in which a woman accidentally leaves behind her purse at a friend's house, which would have signaled in Freudian terms an unconscious intention to return to the friend. In response, Heidegger claims that hypothesizing an unconscious intention such as this enters the realm of *explanation*, which is opposed to phenomenological interpretation dedicated to *describing* the things themselves as they appear. Even though Heidegger understood the *psuche* (mind or spirit) in the Greek sense as fundamentally tied to *phusis* (nature), and Freud is a founding father of the study of the psyche we call "psychology," he seemed to think modern psychology in the vein of Freud was too tied to Cartesian subjectivity; thus, Freudian psychology seemed to be too reliant upon explanation instead of staying true "to the things themselves." He therefore juxtaposed Dasein (human existence) with consciousness in the psychological sense of the term, insisting that Dasein is not equivalent to consciousness.

From the viewpoint of his philosophy, he was right to do so, given that being-in-the-world is built into the being of Dasein, but he didn't seem to be aware that Carl Jung, Freud's one-time protégé, was practicing a version of phenomenological psychology of the unconscious that would have provided another pathway—a *weg*—toward a new understanding of the relationship between humans and nature that could complement other ways, such as found in the poetry of Hebel or Hölderlin, in Eastern traditions like Daoism or Buddhism, or in Eckhart's Christian mysticism. (Heidegger once called his collected works *Wege, nicht Werke*, meaning "paths, not works.") Jung's phenomenological psychology seemed obscure and even occult to many of his contemporaries—the behaviorist B. F. Skinner viewed Jungian psychology as unempirical due to its reliance on the unconscious, and Hans Eysenck, a leading figure of psychology in the latter half of the twentieth century, used Jung's theory of the collective unconscious as an example of an unfalsifiable theory, thus making it unscientific—but recent scientific evidence in evolutionary psychology corroborates key aspects of Jung's findings pertaining to the unconscious. These features are highlighted in *Man and His Symbols*, the very book he was working on while Heidegger was engaging in the Zollikon Seminars.

Along with *Man and His Symbols*, which he had been working on with his close colleagues, Jung had been writing his *Memories, Dreams, Reflections* since 1957, the autobiography released just after his death in 1961, and a work that begins with the claim that his life is a story of the self-realization of the unconscious. The notion of the unconscious dates all the way back to Schelling and arguably even back to Plato, but Freud can be credited with providing the first robust psychological theory of it. In the very same year of the publication of *Logical Investigations*, in which Husserl vows to get "back to the things themselves," Freud, a fellow former student of Brentano, published *The Interpretation of Dreams*, arguing that the unconscious is a powerful force that shapes dreams and other mental phenomena, thus significantly diverging from his mentor who insisted on sticking to describing consciousness.

In Freud's initial account, he argues that dreams are symbolic expressions of unconscious instincts, desires, and repressed thoughts. Eventually, Freud comes to understand the human psyche to be structured in a tripartite way as consisting of (1) the id, which is the primitive, instinctive part that operates according to the pleasure principle, seeking immediate gratification without regard to societal norms or consequences; (2) the superego, the part that acts as a moral compass by keeping these instincts in check and thus aligning the individual with societal norms; and (3) the ego, "a coherent organization of mental processes," as he calls it, that mediates between the two. Jung had become very familiar with Freud's *The Interpretation of Dreams* since he had been asked to review the book by Eugen Bleuler, one of the first academic psychiatrists to take Freud's work on the unconscious seriously; he was also the director of the Burghölzli Hospital's psychiatric clinic, where Jung practiced. In his initial review of Freud, Jung acknowledges Freud's significant contributions to understanding the unconscious via dream interpretation, but he also suggests that Freud had only scratched the surface of the highly complex phenomena related to the unconscious. The two met personally in 1907, and their relationship initially blossomed into a close mentorship, with Freud hailing Jung as his "crown prince" and even his "heir apparent," but Jung eventually came to see Freud to be too narrow-minded: Jung believed that Freud viewed repression—the unconscious defense mechanism that pushes out distressing thoughts, memories, or desires from conscious awareness in order to protect one's ego—as too fundamentally tied to sex and sexuality. Jung recognized several nonsexual factors at play in the process of repression, including an inability to adapt socially or an inability to face the truth about a tragic circumstance that had befallen oneself, among others. Like Aristotle in relation to Plato, Jung had to depart from Freud and go his own way. Truth is more important than friendship.

Rather than separate out the human psyche in terms of id, superego, and ego, Jung outlines the psyche in terms of consciousness being broken into the conscious and the unconscious, with the unconscious comprising both personal *and* collective dimensions, insisting that what we call *psyche* is by no means identical with mere individual consciousness or its contents. Instead, Jung agreed with Aristotle that psyche (*psuche*) is very much a part of nature (*phusis*). While humans have a rational capacity that operates at the level of consciousness, the unconscious is very much operational in our being as well and influences our behavior in various ways. Jung believed that consciousness was no blank slate, a *tabula rasa* as John Locke once famously called it, but rather has been developing via evolution through a slow and laborious process. He defines consciousness as "the relation of psychic contents to the ego insofar as this relation is perceived as such by the ego," with the ego meaning "a complex of ideas which constitutes the center of my field of consciousness."

Right now, your ego is conscious of the content in front of you in these words and the concepts that they signify, but it could very well shift its attention to something else (the feeling of the chair you are sitting on or your feet on the ground perhaps). Human consciousness—when sustained and projected toward a goal—can achieve highly complex tasks; it can even program computers and robots to do tasks more efficiently than the individual human being possibly could, as we have seen in recent years. Although its newest accomplishments as produced through rationalism—in technological advancements like generative artificial intelligence, genetic engineering, and three-dimensional printing, among others—seem to demonstrate a definitive mastery over nature, including human nature, Jung understood that we all retain psychic elements from our distant past in the unconscious that we can never exhaustively master. Indeed, he believed that large swaths of the human mind were still shrouded in darkness at the time of his death, even if he spent much of his life attempting to shed light on the unconscious.

Jung posited that a human develops a persona that is presented to society in order to be recognized as a person, but many of us come to believe that this persona—this *mask*, if we are to be faithful to the original meaning of this word in Latin—is equivalent to our whole being when in fact it is only one side of the psychic coin. The other, darker side of human nature is the aspect he termed the "shadow," which comprises the elements of the human psyche that are refused by the persona or consciousness more generally, "the thing a person has no wish to be," as he once put it. The shadow can be understood at both a personal and a collective level. Personally, the shadow encompasses things about ourselves we find undesirable or socially unacceptable, such as a tendency towards anger, aggression, lust, or other "untoward" desires, as well as repressed memories, feelings, and instincts. Jung defined the "collective" as "all psychic contents that belong not just to one individual but to many, that is, to a society, a people, or to [hu]mankind in general." When viewed in the sense of the collective, the shadow refers to the dark side of the psyche that can ignite a herd mentality and mob behaviors that fuel violence and hatred through, for instance, racist and sexist ideologies or destructive acts like rioting and looting. Failure to acknowledge the shadow on an individual level can lead a person to develop engrained patterns of emotionally charged thoughts and feelings, which Jung called "complexes," such as an inferiority complex in which one perpetually feels less worthy than others, or a superiority complex where someone believes they are better than others. Failure to acknowledge the shadow on a societal level can have catastrophic implications, as seen in Nazi Germany during Jung's lifetime, a movement that would prove damning to Heidegger's legacy in the eyes of many, as he took on the role of Rector of the University of Freiburg shortly after Adolf Hitler became chancellor and attempted to implement *Führerprinzip*, the "Führer principle" in which the university's functions were to align with the Führer's will.

I'll leave it to the reader to come to terms with Heidegger's legacy and its relationship to the shadow. What *is* clear is that Jung believed that it is far healthier to acknowledge the shadow, both in terms of the individual and in terms of the collective, than to repress it, even if it is painful to do so, since it allows for psychic balance and therefore health. For Jung, the activity of the unconscious balances the activity of the conscious. However, many of us ignore or deny the unconscious due to its unpleasant and dark qualities, even though some of those qualities may indeed be better off brought to light. In our own lives, the shadow rears its ugly head occasionally in waking life but mostly in dreams. Sometimes the shadow, representing rejected, denied, or repressed aspects of the self, is personified as a dark, unknown, threatening figure or animal, and sometimes it might appear as a person the dreamer knows but dislikes intensely, since that person embodies qualities the individual denies in oneself. In waking life, we tend to despise individuals that embody traits in ourselves that we find unappealing, such as an inordinate obsession with oneself (an inflated ego that we call "narcissism"). Jungian psychology helps us to look within whenever we experience intense feelings of hatred or jealousy for another, as it can help us to understand our own shadow. The lyrics of a Lumineers song capture this in an inverse way in thinking through a negative first impression: "First we ever met / You thought I was an asshole / Probably correct / But I can see your shadow." The ways in which we are drawn toward or repelled by others is a good gauge for one's comfort level with one's own shadow.

However the shadow appears, Jung insisted that we take a phenomenological approach to dream interpretation and acknowledge the shadow's presence, noting that unconscious aspects of any event can be revealed to us in dreams—not via rational thought, but rather through symbolic images. Jung defines a symbol as "a term, name, or picture that may be familiar in everyday life that possesses specific connotations in addition to its conventional and obvious meaning, implying something vague, unknown, or hidden from us." Common dream symbols can represent archetypes, which are universal, inherited patterns of behavior and personality according to Jung's system of thought. Thus, paying attention to dreams can help us better understand ourselves, even if there is no rational system that could possibly be applied to dream interpretation. Nevertheless, Jung thinks we refuse to acknowledge the significance of dreams because they function in dimensions in time and space that are different than in conscious life. Our insistence on rationality at all costs cuts us off from aspects of ourselves that are spiritual in nature. This refusal of the spiritual, however, is a mistake, since dreams can contain messages that are highly relevant to consciousness in confronting one's own repressed traits or deep emotions regarding one's relationships with others, as well as for recognizing archetypes or patterns of behavior that we have inherited.

Humans who are able to come to terms with both the conscious and the unconscious undergo a process Jung referred to as "individuation," which is explained at length by Jung's collaborator Marie-Louise von Franz in *Man and His Symbols*. The goal of the process of individuation is "the realization of the uniqueness of the individual." In it, the ego does away with all merely egotistic or selfish desires and instead attains "a deeper, more basic form of existence" in which one clearly understands one's purpose in life as connected with nature. Importantly, every single person—you and me and literally everyone else—has a unique purpose that is one's own. But in order to know it, one needs to undergo a conscious coming to terms with the psyche as a whole, both the conscious *and* the unconscious, both the light *and* the dark. This means not only acknowledging one's own unique shadow (Jung called this "the realization of the shadow") but also the dark aspects of human nature on a broader scale (the collective shadow) that manifest themselves in prejudices like racist and sexist ideologies, xenophobic tendencies in which one is fearful of anything different from oneself, and even the outright dehumanization of marginalized groups, as seen in Nazi Germany. An inability to come to terms with the shadow at either a personal level or a collective one results in projection, in which one unconsciously attributes one's own repressed psychological qualities, thoughts, or feelings onto others. Unreflective projection leaves one's life out of balance.

Two relevant archetypes that Jung outlines in *Man and His Symbols* are the *anima* and the *animus*, named in an obvious way to refer to our spiritual animality (*anima* means "spirit" or "soul" in Latin). For Jung, men have "a woman within" that he referred to as the "anima," which includes presumed feminine traits like a capacity for nurturing, intuition, sensitivity, empathy, creativity, gentleness, caring, and emotionality that, if not accepted, can lead to psychological imbalance, insecurities, or an inability to form healthy relationships with others, particularly women. Women, on the other hand, have "a man within" called the "animus," which includes presumed masculine traits like a capacity for leadership, assertiveness, independence, competitiveness, aggression, confidence, strength, and rationality that, if not accepted, can also lead to psychological imbalance, insecurities, or an inability to form healthy relationships with others, particularly men. Acknowledging the anima in a man, or the animus in a woman, awakens a person to one's whole self, thereby leading to, as Franz puts it, "a new spiritual orientation by means of which everything becomes full of life and enterprise," turning life into "a rich, unending inner adventure, full of creative possibilities." In individuation, we meet our anima or our animus, thus making ourselves whole and allowing us to see reality more clearly.

Individuation is Jung's term for the beginning of the process of enlightenment, the very lighting of the dark that Kant referred to as *Aufklärung*, that Siddhartha Gautama called *nirvana*, that Hindu yogis call *moksha*. In Plato's analogy of the cave, the enlightened person is the individual who has escaped the cave and seen the truth who comes back to the mockery of the prisoners who have not seen the light and thus can make no sense of it. Similarly, Nietzsche's character Zarathustra had to overcome the shadow in "the ugliest man" to achieve self-overcoming, thus achieving his final evolution into the overman (*Übermensch*), the highest version of humanity in his framework. Like Plato's escapee, the person who has "seen the light" in Nietzsche's thought is met with ridicule, even though the enlightened person is more aligned with the truth. Understanding that one is aligned with the truth provides the means to *sapere aude*, to "dare to be wise," as Kant informs us in his essay "What Is Enlightenment?," thus having the courage to think for oneself.

In experiencing individuation or the beginning of enlightenment, the self understands that it is intrinsically related to something greater, whether it is conceived as *phusis* in ancient Greece, as *natura* in ancient Rome, as God in medieval times, as God *as* Nature in Spinoza's *Deus sive Natura*, as *Atman* or *anatman* in an Indian context, as the *dao* in ancient China, or as some other suprapersonal entity in other contexts. In his chapter of *Man and His Symbols*, Joseph Henderson provides various versions of the suprapersonal entity across several ancient myths. The way in which individuation occurs is unique to each person and informed by one's culture, but those who experience it have a sense of a renewal of life, a *rejuvenation*, a sense of being "born again." This is why Nietzsche calls the final metamorphosis of the spirit "the child" in *Thus Spake Zarathustra*. It is why Tool's Maynard James Keenan sings, "Join in my child / My shadow moves / Closer to meaning," in a 1996 song of self-discovery echoing Jungian thought.

Whatever one prefers to call it, the beautiful thing about individuation or the initial path toward enlightenment is that it not only gives one's life purpose; it also aligns one's life with the greater whole of nature. It is *natural* for humans to *become what they are* since this is precisely one's *telos*—that is, one's proper end. Heidegger repeatedly argued that *telos* should not be translated as purpose but rather meant "end" for the Greeks, but Jung understood the individuation process to be precisely the means by which one understands one's unique purpose in life. Just as in Aristotle, wherein one's *telos* allows one to achieve *eudaimonia*, achieving individuation allows one to live out one's purpose and thus live a good life. We can frame this in terms of achieving one's full and unique potential by actualizing potential through *arete* (practicing virtue) in the way in which an acorn becomes a flourishing oak tree when nurtured (and natured) accordingly. Here, the words of Hebel as cited by Heidegger align with that of Aristotle and Jung: human *psuche*/psyche/anima/spirit as aligned with *phusis*/nature is a natural unfolding of the whole human—the rational animal—to align with nature more broadly. Jung puts the point the following way: *"There is no difference in principle between organic and psychic growth,"* comparing psychic growth to the growth of a plant. Those among us who have experienced individuation know this, and those among us who are on their way toward individuation, which is literally everyone else, will come to know this as well. It is in your nature.

Jacob Needleman, in his introduction to an English translation of the *Daodejing*, made the astute observation that to be natural in our contemporary context is not easy; indeed, he claimed that we have become such unnatural beings that to be open to our true selves as aligned with nature "is the most difficult thing in the world." Our contemporary, globalized world provides plenty of opportunities to become *distracted*, literally to be put off track, by the spectacle of media and social media on our phones and other devices, thus taking us off the path toward our true nature. Moreover, consumeristic tendencies abound especially in the United States, which has proven to be the most capitalistic country in the world's history, leading humans toward "the giddy whirl" of consumerism that Heidegger connected with nihilism in his Nietzsche volumes. Heidegger recognized that continuing down this track of pervasive *Bessinungslosigkeit*, that is, thoughtlessness, is not only unfulfilling but *dangerous* in his 1955 memorial address, but Jungian individuation informs us that humanity's "main purpose is not to eat, drink, etc., but *to be human*," as Franz informs us.

Combining Heidegger and Jung provides us with a new way, a *weg* or track, to show us that distraction or the consumerism in which one identifies one's being with one's possessions and the nihilism that follows is not inevitable or, to stick with the etymological connection, *intractable*. You are not equivalent to your possessions. A life dedicated to consumerism is a life in which one continually gets what you want but not what you need, to paraphrase Coldplay; in it, you "can't get no (true) satisfaction," if you prefer the language of the Rolling Stones. As Erich Fromm has unquestionably shown, *to have is not to be*. Your purpose is much higher, and your true interests—your *inter-esse* (meaning in Latin "to be between")—can point you down the path (the *tract*) of living a meaningful life. Jung's psychology can help you to trust your intuition and follow your interests, which will inevitably lead to human flourishing.

Even if Heidegger's philosophy and Jung's psychology diverge in important aspects and utilize different language, it appears that Heidegger had an understanding of something akin to individuation in his concept of *Eigentlichkeit*, which is the event of recognizing one's own unique possibilities (*eigen* means "own" in German). For Heidegger, *Eigentlichkeit* occurs amid the backdrop of one's being as *das Man*, the anonymous, everyday way of being where human beings merely blend in and conform to societal norms and expectations. Charles Guignon rightly calls *Eigentlichkeit* "the ideal of owning oneself, of achieving *self-possession*," rather than equating one's self with one's possessions. For Jung, individuation is a processual acceptance of the shadow and a "peeling off" of the mask, the persona that has been formed through socialization to awaken to one's true self. Both have to do with owning one's life as uniquely one's own.

In a 1966 interview with *Der Spiegel* magazine, Heidegger famously said that "only a god can save us" from the trajectory of *Gestell*, thus voicing a pessimism about the possibility of initiating a new paradigm in the human-nature relationship. In his interpretation of Heidegger, Charles Guignon's mentor, Hubert Dreyfus, used "technological nihilism" as the name for the condition of society in which calculative thinking shapes our *entire* understanding of meaning and value, thus plummeting humankind into a technologically sophisticated yet nihilistic world. His collaboration with Sean Kelly, appropriately titled *All Things Shining*, attempts to provide a means to overcome nihilism by cultivating a responsiveness to forces beyond oneself. Another means of awakening the spirit—the anima aspect of the rational animal—is through "shadow work," as Jung calls it, which is the process of becoming aware of and integrating the unconscious shadow into one's conscious existence via Jung's notion of analytical psychology, self-reflection, dream analysis, journaling, and creative expression. Art can also unveil aspects of the unconscious; for example, true musicians who can tap into the human mode of *poiesis* in the original Greek sense of bringing something forth into presence are really tapping into the collective unconscious, thereby revealing aspects of the psyche that might otherwise remain hidden. Attentive listening to music—in the original Greek sense of *musike*, the *techne* or art of the Muses—can be a form of shadow work. William Richardson, the person primarily responsible for introducing Heidegger's thought to the United States, understood this in calling Bob Dylan the spokesman for an entire generation at his lecture at Tulane University in 1966.

Jung informs us that "every concept in our conscious mind has its own psychic associations that vary in intensity either according to the relative importance of the concept to our whole personality, or according to the other ideas and even complexes to which it is associated in our unconscious." Thus, not only the means but the ideational focus of shadow work will vary from person to person. In terms of dream interpretation, if a person has a recurring dream, one should not ignore it but rather consider it to be noteworthy, as the dream is suggesting a means to psychic balance. Jung also informs us that some people find their way through thought and others through feeling; individuation requires awakening both aspects of the human being—the rational and the animal, the thought and the feeling—to become whole. Thus, those who find their way through thought may need to be open to feelings that might be uncomfortable, and those who find their way through feeling might have to engage in thought to complement those feelings.

What is clear is that this process must begin in the individual and that no one can do this work for you, even though a professional psychologist might help with providing tools to do shadow work, or a highly attuned and trustworthy friend might open you up to aspects of yourself that you can come to terms with that might not otherwise be visible to yourself. What we ultimately need to come to terms with is an awakening of the whole psyche, which Jung has shown to be more than merely individual consciousness—and recent evidence in the realm of evolutionary psychology has shown that the human mind is indeed composed of both rational *and* animal/spiritual elements. Thus, the next step is to corroborate Jung's thought with the work of Anthony Stevens, the person who showed that what Eysenck deemed "pseudoscience" due to its lack of falsification is actually corroborated well with the evolutionary history of the human mind. From philosophy to psychology, we must now enter the realm of biology.

Chapter 3
Homo sapiens

In *Man and His Symbols*, Jung warns us that the further we move away from the individual toward abstract ideas about *Homo sapiens*, the more likely we are to fall into error. With that cautionary caveat in mind, we still need to understand the evolutionary trajectory of the human being if we are to understand who we are, since the archetypes—the primitive (*arche*) models (*tupous*)—are still embedded into our psyche. The word *sapiens* in Latin means "wise," which was known as *sophos* to the Greeks; *philosophia*—philosophy—is the love (*philia*) of wisdom (*sophia*). A pearl of wisdom that has been passed down to us from Socrates all the way through Nietzsche in Western philosophy is that you must know thyself (*gnothi seauton*) into order to become what you are (*genoi hoios essi mathon*).

From a Jungian standpoint, knowing your true self means integrating both the conscious aspects and unconscious ones, the latter of which includes personal and collective facets. Jung argued that "just as the human body represents a whole museum of organs, each with a long evolutionary history behind it, so we should expect to find that the mind is organized in a similar way." If he is right, we should expect aspects of the collective unconscious to include vestiges of our evolutionary past. Freud referred to these as "archaic remnants," and Jung calls them simply archetypes. We've already met some archetypes in the anima and the animus, but we can also find similar archetypes in the hero and the villain, concepts that are found in all cultures. The hero embodies courage, strength, and the journey of self-transformation, while the villain embodies the opposite. Regarding the archetypes more broadly speaking, for Jung, "the biological, prehistoric, and unconscious development of the mind in archaic man had a psyche that was still close to that of an animal," but this collective prehistory still informs our human psyche today, even if we tend to follow the Enlightenment thinkers that we are a purely rational entity who has moved beyond our animality. In order to understand the rational animal in its wholeness, to truly *know thyself*, we need to glimpse the evolutionary nature of *Homo sapiens*.

Jung worked as a junior assistant at the Anatomical Institute during the winter semester of 1897–1898, while he was studying medicine at the University of Basel. While there, he informs us that he was "fascinated by the bones of fossil man, particularly by *Neanderthalensis*," the closest extinct human relative, and the then recently discovered *Pithecanthropus* (meaning in Greek simply "ape man") by the Dutch paleoanthropologist Eugène Dubois, which has since been given the Latin name *Homo erectus*. At that point, he was merely twenty-two years old and had already intellectually immersed himself in the philosophies of Kant and Schopenhauer, noting that "the great news of the day," as he put it, was the work of the naturalist Charles Darwin, who had published *On the Origin of Species* a few decades earlier, the work that established the foundations of evolutionary biology.

Darwin had meticulously studied plants and animals—and particularly finches—during his 1831–1836 voyage to the Galapagos Islands, which eventually led him to posit his theory of natural selection. On the islands, he noticed that various species of finches had diverse beak shapes and sizes related to their diets as aligned with specific food sources available on each island. Finches that primarily ate large nuts had strong, thick beaks, while those that primarily ate insects had slender, pointed beaks. Instead of positing that God endowed the different species with different beaks to support their flourishing, Darwin believed that these adaptations were the result of *natural* selection. In the fourth chapter of his monumental work, published in 1859, Darwin outlines how nature "selects" which animals or plants survive, leading him to the ultimate conclusion, shared roughly halfway through the book, that nature operates according to "one general law, leading to the advancement of all organic beings, namely, multiply, vary, let the strongest live and the weakest die." This law has come to be called the "survival of the fittest."

Darwin's theory of natural selection was popularized in Germany by Ernst Haeckel, who modified it to emphasize the role of embryology—the study of *embruon*, which in Greek means "young one" or "that which grows"—in understanding evolution. Haeckel proposed what he referred to as the "biogenetic law" (with *bios* meaning life and *genetic* meaning that which pertains to *genesis*—"origin" or "creation"). The biogenetic law stated that ontogeny, that is, the development of an individual organism, recapitulates phylogeny, that is, the development of a species over evolutionary time (with *ontos* meaning "being" and *phulos* meaning "race" or "tribe"). For Haeckel, this meant that an organism, in the course of its development, goes through all the stages of those forms of life from which it has evolved. For example, a fully-fledged and flourishing butterfly must go through the stages of being a caterpillar, since in its evolutionary history its highest stage was formerly that of a caterpillar. In a letter dated June 9, 1934, to fellow psychologist Gerhard Adler, Jung is explicitly critical of Haeckel's worldview, claiming it to be too enmeshed in rationalism and materialism—the very worldview that we've outlined as being inherited by Descartes and Newton. Nevertheless, he seems to have been inspired by the notion of an evolutionary relationship between ontogeny and phylogeny in his understanding of the development of the human psyche.

In one of Jung's first major works, *Psychology of the Unconscious*, he favorably cites James Mark Baldwin, who was a prominent psychologist in the United States until an apparent sexual indiscretion led to his exile from Johns Hopkins University in 1909 (he was reportedly involved in a sexual scandal that led to his arrest in a Baltimore brothel). Baldwin had been generally ostracized by his American colleagues due to his shattered reputation and lived the remainder of his life in France. Before the apparent scandal, Baldwin published a paper titled "A New Factor in Evolution," in which he attempted to unpack the relationship between ontogeny and phylogeny, both at the biological level and at the psychological level. In it, he argued that psychological evolution and biological evolution "are not two, but one." Essentially, Baldwin believed that the human psyche can adapt to environmental challenges in ways that influence its biology, and thus there existed natural selection through learned behaviors, which essentially meant that humans are not merely biologically determined as some other organisms seem to be. This phenomenon is now called "the Baldwin effect."

The biological anthropologist William Durham provides a helpful explanation of the Baldwin effect in talking through the difference in the percentage of people who display lactose intolerance in northern climates as compared to those in climates closer to the equator. Milk is a good source of vitamin D, which helps with calcium absorption and bone health. Populations of people in northern regions with a long cultural history of dairy farming show significantly less lactose intolerance than their equatorial counterparts, even though dairy farming has been around just as long—if not longer—in those regions. Why? People closer to the equator obtain more of their vitamin D from the sun and thus do not need to complement their bone calcification through milk consumption as extensively as persons in northern climates with less exposure to the sun. Over time, this leads to a greater percentage of lactose intolerance in equatorial populations as genes are passed down from generation to generation. What the Baldwin effect shows is that *the human psyche—through collective, learned behaviors—can influence "biological" natural selection.* This is consistent with our argument, since the human psyche is an aspect of *phusis*, nature.

As the Jungian analyst George Hogenson states, the Baldwin effect showed that "natural selection was no longer natural in the sense of simply responding to the natural environment. It was now a culturally driven natural selection." Learned behaviors via phylogeny can influence the very biological makeup of ontogeny. The cultural practices of our ancestors have informed who we are today, not only culturally but biologically. Jung understood Baldwin's theory to be true. In *Psychology of the Unconscious*, he outlines how the human psyche responds to its environment sometimes merely through instincts, which are compulsory in nature (he defines an instinct as "an impulsion toward certain activities"), but also through other means like intuition, which he defines as an irrational (perceiving) function, through feeling, which he defines as a rational (ordering) function in *Man and His Symbols*, and, of course, through human reason, since we are the rational animal.

As it turns out, recent advancements in gene-editing technologies show promise in human reason's ability to alter human biology in a more direct way, as they allow for extremely precise DNA editing. The Chinese genetic engineer He Jiankui announced in 2018 that he had used the CRISPR-Cas9 gene-editing technique to modify the genes of twin girls with the aim of making them resistant to human immunodeficiency virus (HIV). Current gene-editing technologies especially show promise for what are termed "monogenetic disorders," meaning diseases that are caused by a mutation of a single gene (*mono* simply means "one") like sickle cell disease, cystic fibrosis, or Huntington's disease. The human psyche has various layers and those layers not only can perceive the world but also manipulate aspects of it, including, through the Baldwin effect, human biology over learned behaviors practiced over generations as conditioned by environmental factors, and perhaps in even more efficient ways via gene editing. Jennifer Doudna, the American biochemist who pioneered CRISPR gene-editing technology, is right to urge us toward caution in how we use these technologies, as the implications of their use can change the trajectory of the human species at the biological level.

For our purposes, we need to understand the biological basis of the human psyche as described by Jung, and the person who provided the first robust scientific description of Jung's layered conception of the psyche is Anthony Stevens, a prolific and interdisciplinary thinker who combined psychology, anthropology, medicine, and science. Upon receiving a medical degree from the University of Oxford, Stevens was offered a research fellowship for his doctoral work at the Metera Babies Centre in Athens, Greece, an institution that cared for orphaned infants. The word *metera* in Greek simply means "mother," and the center was set up so that the infants would have substitute mothers in the nurses who would care for them. The standing belief among the vast majority of psychologists at the time aligned with the theory of behaviorism, perpetuated by the likes of Skinner and Eysenck. Skinner's behaviorism was informed by his experiments in operant conditioning, in which learning occurs through modifying behavior in accordance with its consequences. Positive behavior is rewarded and thus repeated, while negative behavior is punished and thus less likely to be repeated by reinforcement; the biological makeup of the individuals under this theory is irrelevant as the behavior simply "operates" according to consequences.

Stevens came to Metera understanding behaviorism, which was the theory of the day, but he was also working under the supervision of John Bowlby, who believed that infants form deep attachments to their mothers as an *evolutionary* survival mechanism. For Bowlby, genetic makeup mattered deeply. If the behaviorists were right and infants' minds come to us as blank slates, it shouldn't have mattered who was feeding and caring for them among the hundred or so nurses at the institute; as long as the appropriate behaviors were rewarded with feedings, the ends should have justified the exchangeable means, which in this case were the substitute mothers. If Bowlby was right, Stevens could expect to find infants forming unique bonds with the individual caretakers, since those particular women were acting as substitute mothers and thus playing that role evolutionarily, so to speak. While there, he found that even though the infants were routinely fed by many nurses, they nearly inevitably formed close attachments to a single or, on rare occasions, a small handful, of women caretakers. In chronicling those relationships, he found that those bonds were forged by nurturing and trust—through physical and social contact, immersion in play, and loving interactions—rather than simply by bottle feeding. This proved to him that behaviorism is flawed: Humans have evolutionary traits just like all other animals and thus are not blank slates that can be programmed via operant conditioning. Bonds in this context were forged by motherly love rather than by mere adherence to scheduled feedings. Any mother, I'm sure, understands this already at a visceral level, as does any aunt who has formed deep relationships with her nieces or nephews.

Stevens's quest to understand the evolutionary reasons behind his findings led him eventually to Jung, who he believed might be able to provide a more robust theory undergirding the architecture of the wide-ranging human psyche than Bowlby, whose specialty was focused on attachment theory, which is now well accepted in psychological circles. He asked his Jungian analyst Irene Champernowne whether his observations at Metera could be corroborated by Jung's notion of the collective unconscious and the archetypes, since he knew she had undergone her own analysis by Jung between 1937 and 1938. Even though Champernowne is now known to us as a pioneer in art therapy, she was also well versed in evolutionary biology and said very plainly to Stevens that archetypes are biological entities that evolved by natural selection. This positive confirmation led Stevens down his path of evolutionary psychology, in which he tried to map Jung's understanding of the psyche onto the evolutionary unfolding of *Homo sapiens*, and particularly the human brain. If Darwin's overarching theory of evolution is correct, we should expect to find evolutionary traces of more primal versions of ourselves embedded in our nature, which is precisely what Jung believed. In describing the rational animal, though, Jung primarily utilized language of philosophy, spirituality, religion, and, of course, psychology, since that was his primary background; although he was clearly familiar with evolutionary science, he was less comfortable in that space and thus didn't use that language.

Stevens, however, was able to bridge Jungian language with the language of science, particularly through ethology, the study of *ethos*, which in Greek is a rich word that is tied to habit, character, custom, and culture, but in this context refers more pointedly to the scientific study of animal behavior (their *ethos*, or habits), focusing on its evolutionary origins. In his undergraduate work at Oxford, Stevens was exposed to Konrad Lorenz's concept of "imprinting" (which explored how young animals form attachments, the theory that influenced his mentor Bowlby) and Nikolaas Tinbergen's work on the importance of both learned *and* innate behavior in animal survival. Bringing this scientific orientation to bear with Jung's more spiritual bent, Stevens argued in *Archetype Revisited*, an update to his 1982 magnum opus, *Archetype: A Natural History of the Self*, that "the theory of archetypes functioning in the collective unconscious of our species is the most important psychological concept to have emerged from the twentieth century and to have persisted into the twenty-first." Stevens's unique contribution was his ability to show us how Jungian archetypes mirror our evolutionary unfolding in scientific language.

To understand Stevens's contribution, we need to gain at least a cursory knowledge of the human brain, while knowing full well that it is one of the most complex structures in the known universe and thus cannot be exhaustively described. Moreover, as the Stanford neuroscientist Andrew Huberman has shown, our brains are plastic, which means we have the ability to change and shape them throughout our entire lives; any neuroscientist knows that pinning down exactly how a human brain works is a deeply challenging task. Nevertheless, we can paint in broad strokes and make sense of the human brain's basic anatomy at a more general level.

The human brain is made up of various layers, all of which must be acknowledged if we are to be considered whole. At its base layer is the reptilian brain, the oldest part of the brain, evolutionarily speaking, and it consists of the brain stem and the cerebellum. This layer of the brain controls basic survival functions like breathing, heart rate, body temperature, and balance, as well as instinctual behaviors like the fight or flight mechanism. Stevens notes that we share the reptilian brain "with all vertebrate creatures," and also that it "has remained remarkably unchanged by the march of evolution." Above and beyond the reptilian brain lies the mammalian brain, also known as the limbic system, the main structures of which are the hippocampus, the amygdala, and the hypothalamus. This layer of the brain primarily houses emotions, memories, habits, and attachments; it is the seat of the snap judgments we make, often unconsciously. The American neuroscientist Paul MacLean argued that three forms of behavior differentiate reptiles from mammals, notably due to the latter's limbic system: (1) nursing and maternal care, (2) audio-vocal communication for maintaining mother-offspring contact via the separation call, and (3) play. Anyone who has watched two squirrels chase each other can see that this behavior is a form of organic play and not simply the act of mechanical automata, as Descartes believed. Opening our eyes to this and similar truths is crucial. MacLean believed that reptilian brain behavior is based primarily around aggression, displays of dominance, and territorial protection. While mammals retain those capacities, they also can engage in more complex behavior with care, communication, and play, due to the limbic system.

The third layer of the brain, the neocortex (*neo* simply means "new" in Latin, and *cortex* means simply "bark," as in the outer layer of a tree), evolved first in primates but then expanded into the human brain as we now know it. As Stevens points out in chapter 13 of *Archetype Revisited*, this portion of the brain is divided into two parts, the cerebral hemispheres, which are "humanity's main claim to fame," noting that "it is the evolutionary development of frontal lobes, coupled with the language areas of the left dominant hemisphere, that has made human civilizations possible." Via the experimental work of Roger Sperry in the 1950s and 1960s, we came to understand that the left hemisphere is primarily concerned with the use of language and with abstract, analytic thought, while the right is more involved in synthesizing sensory data holistically in a Gestalt sort of fashion. The Danish psychologist Edgar Rubin famously showed how this Gestalt shift works through the Rubin vase/face in his ambiguous image.

Thanks to the right hemisphere of your brain, you can recognize the vase by focusing on the black, or you can recognize the profiles of the two faces if focusing on the white. The father of modern neuropsychology, Alexander Luria, contrasted the sequential processing of the left hemisphere with the "simultaneous perceptual processing," as he called it, of the right hemisphere. While the brain is complex and it is probably inaccurate to attribute all logical functions to the left hemisphere and all emotional or intuitive functions and Gestalt processing to the right sphere and the limbic system, it is helpful to distinguish left and right hemispheric functioning, knowing full well that we are painting this picture in broad strokes.

Stevens argues that, as a species, we seem to have collectively projected the dominant functions of our two cerebral hemispheres onto reality inversely such that the left is

associated with darkness and the right is associated with the light. Upon surveying Jung's overarching psychology and the similarities Jung noted between cultures in terms of their symbology, Stevens provides the following table of the archetypal symbolism of right and left (see next page).

The symbolism of right and left, of light and darkness, is no mere accident for Stevens, since this symbolic duality can be seen across cultures, thus suggesting that there is an ontological duality involved that is reflected in the human brain in an inverse way in the left and right hemispheres. In ancient China, the symbol of the *yin* and the *yang* is powerful, with the *yang* referring to light, activity, and the masculine, among others, and the *yin* referring to darkness, receptivity, and the feminine, among others. For the Daoists, the most natural of the ancient Chinese traditions that have been passed down to us, all *qi* (matter-energy) is made up of both *yin* and *yang*, which operate on a spectrum and complement each other; thus symbolic duality mirrors

Right	Left
Good, pure, and sacred	Evil, impure, and profane
Life, medicine, and health	Death, poison, and sickness
Heaven	Hell
Masculinity	Feminitity
Activity	Passivity
The sun	The moon
Daylight	Darkness
Summer	Winter
Joy	Sorrow
Consciousness	Unconsciousness

ontological duality. Harmony in Daoism, *he*, is a matter of finding balance with one's *qi* to achieve *de* (one's unique way of flourishing) as aligned with *dao* (the way of nature).

In India, both Hinduism and Buddhism utilize light and darkness to represent the duality of existence, with enlightenment serving as a means to achieve harmony. The lotus flower is a common symbol in both traditions for enlightenment, as the bright flower emerges from muddy waters. In more Western contexts, while harmony has been a common theme, a more prevalent narrative has been to prioritize the light *over* the darkness, a trait that is shared in some Eastern contexts, though in ways that are typically less prevalent. Zoroastrianism, the ancient Persian religion that serves as a religious base in the West, views the world as a cosmic struggle between lightness (goodness) and darkness (evil), which has informed Judaism, Christianity, and Islam. In both the East and the West, lightness and darkness—whether framed as *yang* and *yin*, the sun and the moon in pagan perspectives, Apollo and Dionysus for the Greeks, or eventually as good and evil in the big three Abrahamic religions—have proven to be culturally significant.

Jung traveled all around the world in his attempt to understand how symbols function similarly across cultures, leading to meetings ranging from the great spiritual leader Ochwiay Biano (Mountain Lake) of the Taos Pueblo in New Mexico to various *laiboni* (shamans) of the Maasai people of Kenya. He also leveraged expertise near his home country by developing a deep intellectual relationship with the German sinologist Richard Wilhelm, who translated several key Daoist and Confucian classical texts into German (some of which Heidegger had familiarity). Stevens takes the factual anthropological data synthesized by Jung and questions how it is related to the biological strata of the human brain. He argues that people seem to differ considerably as to the degree to which the left hemisphere of the brain has come to dominate over the right hemisphere or vice versa. Some of us are deeply detail-oriented and can meticulously engage in logical and analytical thinking to perform tasks, while others are more gifted at synthesizing information as a whole, which is why some persons are better suited as financial analysts or accountants and others find their calling in painting or music. In these respective talents, we see the predominance of the left hemisphere and the right hemisphere, respectively.

Yet we can even see this difference in predominance at a cultural level. Robert Ornstein, the pioneering brain researcher from the United States, argued that the rational thought processes characteristic of Western culture predominantly make use of the left hemisphere, while the intuitive thought processes characteristic of Eastern traditions are more dependent on the right hemisphere. Stevens shows that even if we as individuals or as cultures are predisposed to be right-hemisphere dominant or left-hemisphere dominant, nature has provided a bridge between the hemispheres in the corpus callosum, that is, the tough bundle of fibers connecting them (the word itself means "tough body" in Latin). Eileen Luders has shown that persons who have engaged in mindfulness meditation practices over a long period of time seem to cultivate enhanced brain connectivity between the two hemispheres via the corpus callosum, while individuals who suffer from attention-deficit/hyperactivity disorder (ADHD) have a significantly smaller corpus callosum than individuals without ADHD and thus likely have less holistic brain connectivity. Recent research out of the University of Wisconsin led by Richard Davidson on "interhemispheric transfer," the exchange of information between the two hemispheres, has helped to show that a healthy life entails achieving balance or equilibrium, a sentiment he shares with the Dalai Lama in their dialogue recorded in their 2013 book, *The Mind's Own Physician*. The American neurologist James H. Austin has chronicled the relationship between neuroscience and spirituality in various books that explore the relationship between the brain and Zen Buddhism since his experience of *kensho* in Kyoto in 1974, the name Zen Buddhists use for seeing one's true nature (Jung's word for that is "individuation" in

Man and His Symbols). Luders, Davidson, and Austin have demonstrated things scientifically that have been known to spiritual traditions like Buddhism for centuries. Through them, we come to see that it seems to be the case that the corpus callosum is nature's gift to humanity to enable us see the natural world as it truly is. While we will unpack more relations between science and spirituality later in the book, for now what we are coming to see is that Stevens provides a rough scientific and cultural map for how certain aspects of the brain house certain aspects of the Jungian psyche.

Stevens agrees with neuroscientists like Luders, Davidson, and Austin or spiritual leaders like the Dalai Lama that psychic health is all about balance, and he frames it as balance between the left and the right hemispheres, the light and the dark. Jung believed that these two psychic aspects of the self were incommensurable since one operates according to rationality and the other operates via nonrational means like intuitions and instincts. Nevertheless, he did recognize the possibility of what he termed "mutual toleration" of the light and the dark via the process of individuation, in which "the two opposing 'realities,' the world of the conscious and the world of the unconscious, do not quarrel for supremacy, but each makes the other relative."

Shadow work is helpful in achieving balance, as we learned last chapter, but our societal priorities lean heavily toward one side in the West. Using Jung as his background, Stevens shows how we've engaged in a sort of "cerebral imperialism" in the West in which we have increasingly emphasized left hemispheric functions at the expense of the right, consistent with Ornstein's suggestion. Our preference for certainty, measurable outcomes, and rational thinking has been informed by the rationalist tradition passed down to us from Descartes and Newton. We prioritize these at the expense of intuition, depth, and an openness for ambiguity to allow life to unfold on its own terms. This begins in elementary schools, in which we prioritize language development and logical thinking through reading, mathematics, and science over more intuitive disciplines like art or music. It is no coincidence that the ACT test, a standardized test used for college admission in the United States, is based around a proper understanding of grammar and punctuation in the English language, reading comprehension, and rational-empirical reasoning in the mathematics and science sections; writing, the one opportunity for students to demonstrate an ability to think for themselves and perhaps integrate the logic of the left hemisphere with the intuitive creativity that can accompany the right hemisphere, has become optional.

Recent budget and departmental cuts in American universities, and especially liberal arts colleges, perpetuate this cerebral imperialism in that the first programs typically ousted amid rough financial straits are the arts and the humanities. One Catholic liberal arts college has even engaged in a campaign titled "Preserving the Legacy," which cuts ties with the liberal arts, including theology and religious studies, the very basis of its history, in its attempt to transform into a STEM-based institution aligned with this cerebral imperialism. Other examples abound across the country. The British neuroscientist Iain McGilchrist has hypothesized that our cultural left-brain dominance is creating a meaning crisis in which quantity is valued over quality, and productivity is prioritized over well-being. This is precisely what Hubert Dreyfus understood as technological nihilism, the very concern Heidegger voiced in the dominance of *Gestell* when he uttered those famous lines that "only a god can save us."

Importantly, cerebral imperialism is not merely a historical effect of the supposed Cartesian/Newtonian "triumph" of reason over emotion; rather, this imperialism is exacerbated by persons in power in highly sophisticated ways through ideational manipulation that exploits the weaknesses or ignorance surrounding the darker aspects of the brain. The initial masters of powerful ideational manipulation, to my mind, were the Nazis. In *Mein Kampf*, Adolf Hitler outlines how "the broad masses of a nation are always more easily corrupted in the deeper strata of their emotional nature," essentially making it plainly obvious that propaganda is a matter of exploiting the aspects of the human brain that are less developed or more primal, the aspects Stevens outlined as lying in the reptilian, limbic, and right hemispheric aspects of the brain. Subliminal messaging is directed toward the aspect of the brain *below* the limbic system (*sub* means "under," "beneath," or "below" in Latin), that is, the reptilian brain that is largely governed by instinct, but this form of messaging is also directed beneath the threshold (*limen* means "threshold" in Latin) of rational consciousness more broadly, that is, the darker aspects of the brain. In a 1928 speech to his fellow Nazi party members titled "Knowledge and Propaganda," Joseph Goebbels, Hitler's master of propaganda, outlines the Nazi approach to propaganda, stating that the measure of good propaganda has nothing to do with the truth of the matter, but rather in whether "it can win over and fire up people for an idea." He states very plainly that knowledge in this sphere just *is* the power to transmit the idea *of the powerful* onto the masses, thereby gaining *power over* them, and the means to do so are through appealing to emotions using simple, repeated slogans that target the prejudices of the masses.

When well crafted, propaganda can convince persons of wildly outlandish notions that whole populations of persons are subhuman and deserve to be totally annihilated, as Hitler's *Vernichtungskrieg*, his war of extermination, showed us. Although Hitler envisioned a Thousand-Year Reich as his ideas gained ground and as he amassed global power, it is fitting that he died underground by suicide and thus symbolically in the dark, in the *Führerbunker* a mere twelve years after his initial rise to power—a fate that befell Goebbels and his family the very next day. Both tried to manipulate human beings in ways that stifled human flourishing as it naturally should unfold by trying to create the world in their dark image, but nature, including human nature, cannot ultimately be steered by human beings, much less a single deranged human being and his henchman propagandist.

Anyone who has visited the former concentration and extermination camps in Auschwitz, Dachau, Stutthof, and others can sense the profound unnaturalness of the environments, as they are the extreme result of ideational manipulation. We do well to remind ourselves that just east of the Stutthof Concentration Camp Museum, which still houses its original gas chamber, is where Kant penned his motto of the Enlightenment, *sapere aude*, "dare to be wise," with *sapientia*, wisdom, being understood as the ultimate natural end (*telos*) of *Homo sapiens*.

In ways much less extreme than the ideational manipulation of the Nazis, contemporary humans are still besieged daily with ideational manipulation that exploits the cerebral imperialism of the left hemisphere through advertising, social media, mass media, and government rhetoric, among other channels. Techniques of subliminal messaging help to drive the consumerism and the distraction of social media mentioned in the last chapter. Luxury brands have done this by carefully showcasing beautiful people in their advertisements, thereby activating the pleasure principle in their targeted audiences, rather than simply laying out the rational reasons as to why their product is better than like products; this tactic has now been employed by social media influencers as well. Even realms that are not mere-ly about social status but more directly related to human health have succumbed to these strategies. Direct-to-consumer pharmaceutical advertisements in the United States, for instance, utilize mixed messaging techniques that exploit the human tendency to focus on the visual over the verbal when the content is discordant.

Moreover, increasingly sophisticated means are now available to nudge consumer behavior in certain directions, such as algorithmic suggestions based on the preferences of the individual or scarcity tactics that create a sense of urgency on the part of the consumer, like "limited time only" promotions. A common tactic is to craft the message in a way that seems as if it is directed specifically to the individual, as seen in the famous "I WANT YOU" poster of Uncle Sam propagated in the United States during World War I. Specific political uses of these tactics today are too obvious to mention, especially in aspects of American politics that have prioritized *le spectacle de l'excès*, that is, "the spectacle of excess," in Roland Barthes's sense of over-the-top, theatrical performances meant to emotionally charge the audience rather than mind any respect for the truth, thus aligning their brash antics with the cartoonish personalities that abound in professional wrestling, tapping into the Jungian archetypes of the hero and the villain.

When this is coupled with the corporate capitalism that has shaped the United States, it breeds Rage Against the Machine; when those exploitive tactics include framing minorities as subhuman, it breeds Niggaz Wit Attitudes (N.W.A.). Generally speaking, these tactics prop up "the vile maxim of the masters of [hu]mankind," as Adam Smith called it, which is "all for ourselves, and nothing for other people" by those in power. Evan Osnos has chronicled how our current "masters of [hu]mankind," the ultra-wealthy, are simultaneously spending their leisure on giga-yachts that are larger than American football fields while building elaborate doomsday prep bunkers in preparation of societal collapse. All this occurs while the majority of us live merely in the spectacle, which Debord rightly called "a social relation among people mediated by images" that cuts us off from reality as it truly is.

Perhaps the biggest propaganda campaign in the history of the human species, though, has been related to anthropogenic climate change, which threatens human civilizations as we have come to know them. James Hansen was the first scientist to publicly explain the potential dangers of climate change to the US Senate—on June 23, 1988. His testimony made front-page news, as *The New York Times*, America's democratic pulse, began the June 24th edition with the headline, "Global Warming Has Begun, Expert Tells Senate." Unsurprisingly, America's capitalistic pulse of information, *The Wall Street Journal*, did not cover Hansen's testimony at all on the front page. Humanity, broadly speaking, sided with *The Wall Street Journal*, since modern societal infrastructures have been formed around fossil fuels since the Industrial Revolution.

This initial denial, however, is not necessarily our fault. Naomi Oreskes and Erik Conway have demonstrated how fossil fuel industries have employed propaganda tactics to sow doubt and confusion about the status of climate change, thereby generating "merchants of doubt" who gained power and wealth as a result of these tactics. Given how deeply embedded fossil fuels have become in the global energy system, that factitious skepticism has been perpetuated by politicians and other persons in power, leading us to the precarious situation we now face as *Homo sapiens*, in which human civilizations as we have come to know them are put at risk. Greta Thunberg understood that the only appropriate question to ask the powerful who have perpetuated these falsities is "How dare you?"

Scientifically, we know the status of anthropogenic climate change and can roughly predict the way in which future human life on the planet will unfold thanks to the Intergovernmental Panel on Climate Change, the largest peer-reviewed scientific collaboration in the history of the world, with its reports initially published in 1990 and updated regularly since then. Even if Hansen's testimony did not shift society writ large, it did place us on a path to understand the truth scientifically. However, everything depends on how we respond to this knowledge, a response that requires nothing less than *colossal* thinking, that is, thinking that integrates the left hemisphere with the right hemisphere while acknowledging the influence of our reptilian and mammalian past. If we continue to perpetuate American Disenlightenment, in Martin Schönfeld's sense the term—an age marked by anti-intellectualism, authoritarian tendencies, and the devaluation of the humanities— we will continue to be crippled by cerebral imperialism and thus continue to fall prey to the vile maxim of the masters of humankind, all while embracing technological nihilism. You and I can do better than this. If we dare to engage in colossal thinking, we may very well be able to *sapere aude*, to dare to be wise, and initiate *colossal wisdom, colossophia*, in which our knowledge bleeds into our behavior, thus steering the civilizational ship in the right direction while coming to know thyself and earning our rightful name as *Homo sapiens*.

Chapter 4
Wounded Gaia

Your beautiful human brain is capable of brilliant things when it is used to its full capacity. There are, however, forces beyond you holding you back. It is time to recognize those forces that assault you on all fronts—emotionally, spiritually, politically, and through other means. The classical work *Propaganda* by Edward Bernays, a nephew of Freud, is a helpful tool in this regard. What you and I need to do most, though, as a complement to that work, is to understand your rightful place in the natural world. Since ancient times, humans have understood themselves as an intersection of various spheres and symbolized that nexus with an "X" or a cross. This symbol has been relevant in both Eastern and Western contexts. The Nazis misappropriated the symbol of the swastika, which in Sanskrit means "well-being," an apt translation for Aristotle's notion of *eudaimonia*, toward entirely unnatural means. That symbol will now forever be marked by hatred and must be abandoned, even though in ancient contexts it symbolized the balance and wholeness we are seeking. We need a way to symbolize the human place in nature, since humans are symbolic beings. Jung informs us that the first Christians used the following symbol to signify the nature of human beings.

This symbol has come to be called the *crux immissa quadrata*, the cross with four equal lengths. Eventually, as *contemptus mundi* (contempt of the material world) took

over in the West, the center of the cross moved upward to signify that humans are made *imago Dei*, in the image or likeness of God, and thus above the rest of merely carnal creation. In his 1967 paper, Lynn White Jr. showed how that anthropocentric ideology has played out historically. Ironically, our supposedly spiritually based high-mindedness of manifest destiny (marked by a frontier mentality and global capitalism) has wrought material destruction while simultaneously cutting us off from our true spirituality. Even if the rational animal has sought to discard our animality, we are, in the end, human, all too human. In the West, if anything, we need to bracket our rationality at times and get back in touch with our *anima* or spirit. Your uniquely creative interests are the guide for what that needs to look like for you as an individual.

What does the square cross represent? The answer to that question depends on the cultural context. From a biological perspective, though, we can recognize truth in this symbol in that the human being, an instantiation of nature in the biosphere, is simultaneously enmeshed in the inter-workings of the hydrosphere, the geosphere, and the atmosphere. We exist, that is, at the nexus of the four great systems of the earth. Water is the source of all life, and thus a human being who lacks water will inevitably die, thus showing our vital connection to the hydrosphere. The geosphere encompasses all rocks and minerals, a realm equally important to human flourishing. We've seen already how the human body needs the mineral calcium to maintain a healthy bone structure. The earth supplies similar minerals crucial to human health like phosphorus, which aids in energy production and cell repair, as well as magnesium, sodium, and potassium to maintain normal nerve and muscle function, among others. The biosphere, hydrosphere, and geosphere all interact with the atmosphere, the gaseous layer surrounding Earth that is primarily composed of nitrogen and oxygen, the very layer that provides the air we breathe and that protects us from solar radiation. Put together, the square cross signifies the human being as a nexus in a vast circuit of relationships that operate simultaneously and interdependently. To maintain human health, we need clean water, healthy food (that is, food rich with micronutrients and minerals, the inorganic elements derived from soil and water, and vitamins, the organic compounds produced by plants and animals), and clean air to breathe. Given our evolutionary makeup as *bios*, as life, we cannot function without these conditions. If these get threatened, we cannot help but to get up and stand up and fight for these natural rights, to paraphrase Bob Marley. And for many this is no mere abstraction. Individuals living in failed states marked by a breakdown of governance so extensive that there is an inability to provide for basic human needs know this all too well.

We need basic resources to survive, and those resources flow through the four main systems. Humans, though, through our collective arrogant rationality, have assaulted all four of these systems since the onset of the Anthropocene, the era marked by global influences of *anthropos*, the Greek name for human being. Our assault on the biosphere happens in both direct and indirect ways. Directly, we have hunted various species of animals to the point of extinction, from the gentle dodo bird to the mighty woolly mammoth. The de-extinction project led by Colossal Biosciences is trying to bring back a hybrid version of the woolly mammoth utilizing Asian elephant genes and the dodo bird using Nicobar pigeons, though this doesn't detract from the fact that humans caused their extinction in the first place. Indirectly, we have engaged in extensive terra-transformation, a remaking of the earth in our own modern image through the creation of cities and the transportation infrastructures that connect them, which has fragmented the habitats of countless species, forcing extinction in some cases and leaving others, even some highly sophisticated ones like the Sumatran orangutan, which evolutionarily are closely related to us (*orangutan* means "forest person"), on the brink of extinction. We are now living in the midst of the Sixth Extinction, a rapid decline in biodiversity driven primarily by human beings. Elizabeth Kolbert provides a fitting narrative of that story in her "unnatural history."

Our assault on the hydrosphere is also very real and tied to our assault on the biosphere. One of the most obvious means of terra-transformation is modern agriculture, which has affected our biospheric systems with fertilizers, pesticides, and livestock waste. Agricultural runoff and nutrient pollution, when combined with industrial pollution and chemical waste, have created hypoxic zones—that is, "dead zones," meaning places that were formally teeming with life (*bios*) but can no longer serve that end due to human-induced conditions. This is glaringly obvious in the Gulf of Mexico, in which there is a dead zone that was roughly the size of Connecticut in 2025 due to the massive pollution related to agricultural practices that flood down the Mississippi River. West of there lies the so-called Great Pacific Garbage Patch, an accumulation of trillions of pieces of plastic that can be easily seen on a flight from California to Hawaii. Corine Pelluchon has brilliantly chronicled our assault on the hydrosphere in her ecological-existential approach.

Our assault on the geosphere is no less startling, which began with the onset of fossil fuel extraction during the Industrial Revolution and has been accelerated by more efficient means to extract oil and gas through hydraulic fracturing technologies and both surface (via strip mining and mountaintop removal) and subsurface (underground) mining techniques to access coal, the dirtiest of all the fossil fuels. The American physicist Amory Lovins rightly notes that while "fire made us human, fossil fuels made us modern." As we continue to burn these fossil fuels, we change the very makeup of the atmosphere. Anthropogenic climate change is a perfect example of the ways in which the earth systems interact. Through advances in geology using the very scientific methods unleashed to us by the likes of Bacon, Descartes, and Newton, *bios* in the form of humans have learned to mine the geosphere for its fossil fuels as a source of energy. The very burning of these fuels, however, can't help but release carbon dioxide, a major greenhouse gas, into the atmosphere, trapping heat and warming the planet's climate. This carbon dioxide is also absorbed by the hydrosphere, leading to ocean acidification, which harms *bios* in the form of marine life, especially life that forms shells and skeletons and the various marine life-forms that rely upon coral reefs for their habitats. The biosphere more broadly has been put at risk, as our altered planet is changing faster than some biospheric species can adapt. On the whole, our alteration of the geosphere cannot help but influence the biosphere, hydrosphere, and atmosphere, since everything is connected.

Even if the public didn't heed James Hansen's warnings on the science of climate change after his testimonial on June 23, 1988, the scientific community did. The response was the creation of the Intergovernmental Panel on Climate Change (IPCC), the largest peer-reviewed scientific collaboration in the history of humankind, which published the first Assessment Report in 1990 confirming the existence of a natural greenhouse effect; it stated in plain language that human activities were significantly increasing the atmospheric conditions of greenhouse gases. In the Sixth Assessment Report, published in 2023, the IPCC outlined five "Shared Socioeconomic Pathways" (SSPs) to show how humans will likely fare, given how we respond to the science. In the most optimistic scenario, dubbed SSP1-1.9, we prioritize net-zero carbon dioxide emissions around mid-century, thereby righting the global civilizational ship back toward environmental sustainability, even if we cannot undo some of the damage that is already done. In that setting, the global mean surface temperature is roughly 60 degrees Fahrenheit (15.5 degrees Celsius), only a few degrees above what it was just before the Industrial Revolution.

Unfortunately, that scenario is unlikely, since roughly 80 percent of the world's energy consumption still revolves around fossil fuels. In the most pessimistic scenario, dubbed SSP5-8.5, we adopt a "business as usual" approach that aligns with rapid economic growth fueled by fossil fuels and uncurbed by any climate policies; this scenario leads to very high greenhouse gas emissions and a temperature increase that could range between around 6 and 10 degrees Fahrenheit globally on average by 2100, the year my daughter is set to turn eighty-five years old and my sons are set to turn eighty-four and eighty-two, respectively. If that scenario unfolds, none of them make it that far and neither do any of your loved ones, as human civilizations as we have come to know them will have already collapsed. The image of their premature corpses is enough for me to help shift the world in the right direction. The natural response to that image is not Stoic *ataraxia* but rather *horror*. Even if the left-brain scientific knowledge is clear, it is the right-brain emotional knowledge that needs to be activated to come to terms with our predicament.

The issue, actually, isn't only about my kids or the fate of your loved ones in the future; it is about *you and me, here and now*. We are already seeing rising sea levels and more frequent and intense heat waves that not only turn people into climate refugees but also seriously threaten human health. Some of the most vulnerable countries in the Pacific islands, like Tuvalu, Kiribata, and others, have already invested significant resources and energy into their resettlement strategies. The issue, though, is not merely about vulnerable populations in especially fragile geographical locations. The last decade is easily the warmest on record, which has resulted in increased wildfires that threaten food security and exacerbate heat-related illnesses like respiratory problems from poor air quality. Moreover, additional atmospheric energy shifts precipitation patterns in disparate ways, as some communities experience more intense rain and flooding while others face prolonged droughts.

The masters of humankind can no longer hide what is there for all of us to see. Right now, the richest 1 percent of the world's population owns roughly half of all global wealth, and they seem dead set on continuing to funnel it in their direction, using propaganda as they increasingly own media outlets and leverage like-minded entities with deep pockets in ways that are reminiscent of Nazi Germany. Back then, industrialists like Fritz Thyssen, head of the German Iron and Steel Industry Association, and Gustav Krupp von Bohlen und Halbach, the head of the weapons manufacturing firm that funded the *Wehrmacht*, the Nazi war machine, profited massively from the Nazi movement. Anyone with their eyes open can see that the same playbook is being applied in America today, with the help of foreign sources, a technique the Nazis also enacted. The bulk of this strategy at the political level aligns with Niccolo Machiavelli's *The Prince*, in which the ruler is willing to do whatever is necessary, including morally questionable acts, to maintain power, since the end always justifies the means in that framework.

Humans, though, can't help but wake up, as that is our proper nature. During the French Revolution, King Louis XVI's overreach of power led to his premature death at the age of thirty-eight by the guillotine, and Hitler died in a bunker with his mistress at the age of fifty-six. Hitler's fate was influenced by Americans like my grandfather, then a poor farm boy from Wisconsin, who took up the role of medic and stormed the beaches of Normandy on June 6, 1944, to help turn the tides of World War II. Our doomsday is no different, but the stakes are even higher this time as the fate of human life on planet Earth is in the balance.

How do we respond? First, we need to come to terms with the reality of our predicament. Albert Camus, in *The Rebel*, rightly called this the confrontation of an order of things that oppresses you with "the insistence on a kind of right not to be oppressed beyond the limit that you can tolerate." That word, "limit," is absolutely crucial. You and I have limits to our toleration of oppression, just as humanity itself has natural built-in limits that we cannot surpass if we are to maintain a continued existence. The Greeks understood limit as *peras*, and it is etymologically tied to the word "parameter." A 2009 article authored by Johan Rockström of the Potsdam Institute for Climate Impact Research and coauthored by the likes of James Hansen and the atmospheric chemist Paul Crutzen (the person responsible for popularizing the term "Anthropocene") outlined the parameters for the survival of the human species as a "safe operating space for humanity." That article is, to my mind, the most important paper of the twenty-first century thus far.

In it, they summarize how the Earth is essentially a life-support system for all members of the biosphere, that is, people, animals, and plants. However, human activities—via pollution in the form of fossil fuel emissions and through other means, deforestation, and overconsumption of natural resources—put that system in danger. Essentially, the authors ask how much damage the Earth can take before things get really, really bad, listing nine systems that help keep the Earth system stable enough to support human civilizations as we have come to know them. The three primary threats to civilizational stability listed at the time were anthropogenic climate change, the loss of biospheric integrity, which is the scientific way of framing the Sixth Extinction, and the excessive human introduction of nitrogen into the environment via the overuse of agricultural fertilizers. In a more recent paper from 2023 published in *Science Advances*, we are informed that six of the nine systems have now been pushed beyond their safe operating spaces, as land-system change via terra-transformations of deforestation and urbanization have increased (the fourth system), leading to an overuse of freshwater resources for agriculture, industry, and cities (the fifth system). Moreover, we continue to introduce synthetic substances like plastics and pesticides into the natural environment at a rate that is faster than nature can process them (the sixth system). All of this leads us to *terra precarium*, a precarious planet for the human species.

The bad news is that once we go too far beyond the parameters of any of these systems, it will trigger nonlinear, abrupt, and catastrophic change due to the way in which these systems work. We get our word system from the Greek word *sustema*, which combines *sun*, meaning "together," and *istemi*, meaning "to stand." Thus, a system is an organized whole that stands together. The first person to provide a logic of systems, a "systemology," in the Western world was Ludwig von Bertalanffy, a brilliant interdisciplinary thinker who, like Heidegger, got caught up in the Nazi movement. Bertalanffy initially studied philosophy but eventually became a biologist. His general systems theory is ultimately a philosophy of biology. Bertalanffy argued that there are two types of systems: closed systems that do not interact with their environment, and open systems that do. Your sealed thermos bottle of hot coffee functions partially as a closed system by preventing the coffee from spilling, even if it ultimately allows for heat transfer through its walls. Living systems do not function like the walls of a thermos that prevent the coffee spill but rather function in an open fashion and, in an open system, *the whole is always more than the sum of its parts.*

The human body functions as an overarching system made up of embedded and interconnected systems like the respiratory and circulatory systems. A class in anatomy and physiology provides the means for a person to understand the relationships between the human body as a whole and its various parts. In a healthy body, the systems function together. For instance, the respiratory system brings oxygen to the body via the lungs, and the circulatory system transports that oxygen to cells via the heart and blood vessels while also carrying carbon dioxide, a waste product of cellular activity, back out of the body through the respiratory system. If the heart stops working or the lungs cease to perform their vital function, the system fails. Even though humans have created machines in ventilators to help people breathe when they can't do it effectively on their own, this doesn't change the fact that the system's operation is contingent upon certain conditions and laws.

Just as the body requires various interconnected systems to work together to allow for flourishing, so does Earth as a planet collectively. The primary spheres of the earth system are the geosphere pertaining to *geo*, the ground; the hydrosphere pertaining to *hydro*, water; the biosphere pertaining to *bios*, life; and the atmosphere pertaining to *atmos*, gas. The interconnections between these systems result in the earth system more broadly. James Lovelock's Gaia hypothesis posits that the Earth is a self-regulating, complex system that comprises all of these spheres in a way no different than the way in which your body comprises the various systems to promote your health. Systems exist within systems, and Gaia is the name for the earth system on the broadest level. Right now, Gaia is severely wounded. In order to heal it, we have work to do.

In the West, our understanding of Gaia systematically as *phusis*, nature, began with Aristotle, whose *Physics* forms the basis of Western scientific thought. In that work, Aristotle argues that there must be *logoi*, basic principles, at work (*ergon*) in nature (*phusis*). The human, as the *zoon logon echon*, the animal having *logos*, can make an account of the transformations of energy (*en-ergon*), with energy simply meaning "in work." *Phusis* is processual in Aristotle's account, with all change involving an entity coming to be from out of its opposite; order comes from chaos or, put in a different way, the light emerges from the dark. All physical entities are a combination of matter (*hule*) and form (*eidos*) for Aristotle. All matter has work to do, meaning we are all *en-ergon*, in the process of working toward our *telos*, our proper end. An acorn has principles within it (*logoi*) that allow it to flourish properly into an oak tree. However, in order for it to do so, it needs proper conditions to grow (e.g., a fitting environment with appropriate amounts of water, sunlight, and nutrients). Moreover, the oak tree has a natural limit, its *peras*. Oak trees can grow in my home state of Wisconsin but not in sub-Saharan Africa, since the parameters for their growth do not exist there. Viewed collectively, a healthy forest with solid oak trees flourishes because those conditions are met.

Humans, too, have principles within us to allow us to flourish and become ourselves, but we also need proper conditions to achieve *eudaimonia*, a good life. Yet those very conditions are being threatened by none other than ourselves, and especially by the masters of humankind. Anthropogenic climate change specifically and literally threatens those conditions, thereby putting us at risk in the same way that a lit match threatens the oak trees in the forest. Climate change has been smoldering since the onset of the Industrial Revolution, powered by Newtonian physics, when we learned to harness the energies of dead animals in fossil fuels. But this smoldering has turned to flame with the increased population growth of humans, who have increasingly adopted the mode of hyperconsumeristic living.

Scientifically, we know the earth is a giant self-regulating system in which the living and nonliving parts interact to maintain conditions suitable for life. As in any open system, feedback loops keep the system in balance (just as the lungs increase the rate of breath when signaled by an increase of carbon dioxide by chemoreceptors in the brain and the cardiovascular system), but human activity has audaciously pushed some of these out of balance. One such feedback loop is the albedo effect, a positive feedback loop in the context of climate change. Climate change means the Earth is warming up, which means the white parts (ice and snow) that reflect sunlight back into space are melting and turning into darker surfaces, like the ocean or land surfaces, that do not reflect sunlight as well. As these darker surfaces absorb more heat from the sun, the Earth becomes even warmer, thus increasing the rate at which all of this occurs. Eventually, on the path we are on, we will reach a tipping point that will result in cataclysmic decline. Similar feedback loops can be found in the relationship between the hydrosphere and atmosphere in terms of water-vapor feedback, ocean circulation changes, and more broadly carbon-cycle feedback—which affects all earth systems.

The physicist Peter Jeanmaire has shown how what Hölderlin termed "the firm law" is the rulebook of nature that accompanies the law of gravitation, the laws of thermodynamics, and the increasingly understood laws in emerging systems theory that pertain to self-organization (the process where a system develops order and structure), bipolarity (the two opposing but complementary forces at work in any system), nonlinearity (where energy input and energy outputs are not proportional), and attractors (the point at which the system inevitably tends). As with the parameters within which all life-forms must abide, these are rules that cannot be broken without dire consequence. The great American scientist E. O. Wilson stated plainly in 2002 that the constraints of the biosphere are fixed and that the bottleneck through which we are passing is real. To heal Gaia, which is to save ourselves, we must realign ourselves with these parameters, in ourselves and with the earth—and a new sense of spirituality, of interconnectedness, provides an answer.

In Newton's system, the earth is seen as a giant billiard table with strict laws. As it turns out, though, the earth is not a cold, dead place, as Explosions in the Sky beautifully reminds us. It is time for us, here and now, to breathe life back into wounded Gaia and become the rational animal— by becoming spiritual again. In order to do so, we need to open up our eyes and see the truth about ourselves and the earth. We need to see ourselves as part of Gaia and not separate from it. Ultimately, this requires a shift in our sense of identity: as a rational animal, we are individuals but never wholly individual as our very existence relies upon Gaia's health. We need to recognize ourselves as foci in the ultimate field of Gaia. In that context, we need to recognize that there is no focus without the field and no field without the focus. This paradigm shift in the human understanding of its relationship with nature follows the words of Stu Mackenzie of King Gizzard and the Lizard Wizard: "I am God / I am you / I am me / I am Gaia." Before, he continues, "Gaia bequeaths / Dirt is deceased / Gaia dies / No one sees." We are Gaia.

We have reached wake-up time, in Tom Petty's sense, the "time to open up your eyes—and rise—and shine." Some of us have shadow work to do in order to get there; others are already beginning to see things clearly. Some of us approach the human-nature relationship on a secular level, and others approach it on a spiritual level. Gaia needs all of us to right the civilizational ship. But in this new spirituality, however we each realize it in our own individuation, the earth must be viewed as sacred, relational, and alive. Ironically, in the West, this brings us back to not Aristotle but Plato, our most metaphysical thinker who at one point spoke of the soul of the world, rendered as the *psuche tou kos-*

mos (the soul of the cosmos) or the *psyche tou pantos* (the soul that permeates all). In Latin, this came to be called the *anima mundi*, the world soul. The doctrine of *contemptus mundi* (contempt of the world) that overtook *anima mundi* has severed our true relationship with Earth, leading to our current ecocrisis. Instead of contempt of the natural world, we need to build a spiritual connection with it. This requires us to overcome technological nihilism and see through the propaganda tactics of the masters of humankind in order to see the truth about the precarity of our global situation and prioritize getting back to the safe operating spaces of the great earth systems.

Spirituality is a vague and sometimes denigrated topic, but at its heart it has to do with awakening the breath that begets life, the anima/*psuche*/psyche, that is, the whole self. While this is not necessarily a religious undertaking, it requires the sort of devotion that we find in religious contexts. Moreover, religion itself can help. Every single major Western religion can serve as a means to shift us in the right direction, but it depends on what we prioritize. In my home country of the United States, roughly two in three adults still identify as Christians. There are thinkers in this tradition that have seen the light, including most obviously Jesus of Nazareth, who became "the way and the truth and the life," but also Meister Eckhart of Germany, Saint Francis of Assisi of Italy, and Pierre Teilhard de Chardin of France. If you are truly Christian and combine that faith with a spirit of *sapere aude*, thus daring to be wise and having the courage to think for yourself, you will undoubtedly see the light as well. If you lead a congregation, you must lead toward the truth and not toward merely profit if you are seeking genuine spiritual nourishment for your people. Jesus, after all, lived a simple life, by all accounts we have of his carnal existence. In Judaism, Moses de León of Spain, as well as Isaac Luria, hailing from the holiest city in Jerusalem, can help to show the way. Both thinkers provide an understanding of the human place in the cosmos. Luria's conception of *tikkun olam*, that is, repair of the world, is especially pertinent. In Islam, it is, of course, blasphemous to point to anything other than the Qur'an, but key spiritual figures in Sufism like Rabia al-Adawiyya, al-Hallaj, and Ibn Arabi may prove helpful in the Muslim quest for enlightenment. Every single one of these traditions shows that humans are interconnected with every other living entity in a complex system and related to a larger entity known by various names but ultimately pointing to the divine.

Everyone's spiritual journey will be different but should be informed by what is salient to the individual. My own spiritual journey led me to the East half my lifetime ago. While in China during the summer of 2005, I climbed the holiest mountain of Daoism, Mount Tai (Taishan), and visited the grave of Kongzi, in Qufu. Those traditions of Daoism and Confucianism have played a pivotal part in my own trajectory ever since, so I want to end this chapter by sharing the wisdom I've learned from those spheres in case my psychic wavelengths jibe with your own. Though everyone's path will be different, our goal, our end, our *telos* is in making ourselves whole—within ourselves and with the earth.

The two primary texts of the Daoist tradition are the *Daodejing* and the *Zhuangzi*, the first of which describes the nature of reality and the second of which shows you how to move from a *xiaoren*, a small person, to a *zhenren*, a true person who embodies the *dao* and lives in accordance with its natural principles. The *Daodejing* is ultimately a manual for leaders, but in it we also glimpse the nature of reality since leaders were trained to follow the *dao* if they were to successfully lead their people. Although the ultimate reality—called *tian* in China—cannot be exhaustively known by humans, its structure is knowable and its pulse is undeniable when felt. The *dao* is the way of nature, and the *dao* is informed by all *de*, the various foci that make up its network. You and I are instantiated foci, *de*, and our ability to flourish is contingent upon our ability to align with the *dao*. All *de* are intrinsically related with one another, but none of us are static entities, as we all are meant to grow in our own unique ways. Growth requires an attitude of openness to be informed by others. Just as a flower needs space to grow, so do your own unique traits. As humans, we grow bodily but also spiritually as we groove into our unique character traits. A fitting analogy for the plasticity of character in China is to be like bamboo, which is firm but bendable.

Roger Ames and David Hall, two of the best interpreters of Daoism in the Western world, describe the *dao* as the discernible rhythm and regularity of the world as it unfolds around us and through us. This rhythm fluctuates in each *de* and its relationships with other focal points through *qi*, the spectrum of matter-energy that permeates the world. All *qi* is a combination of *yang*, the light, and *yin*, the dark, two forces that are opposing yet complementary at the same time. One can think of the *yang* as a mountain, but there is no mountain without a valley, the *yin*. Some of us are predisposed to be more *yang* than *yin*, while others are predisposed to be more *yin* than *yang*. In order to flourish, we need to achieve *he*, harmony, not only in terms of our own *qi*, thereby achieving *yinyang*, but also in terms of relating to the *qi* of those around us.

Harmony can be achieved between two persons when they fully understand each other and complement each other; in some cases, "opposites attract." Some of you have found this complementary force in another person or even an animal one finds especially endearing, thus helping to make one whole, and others will awaken their anima or an-

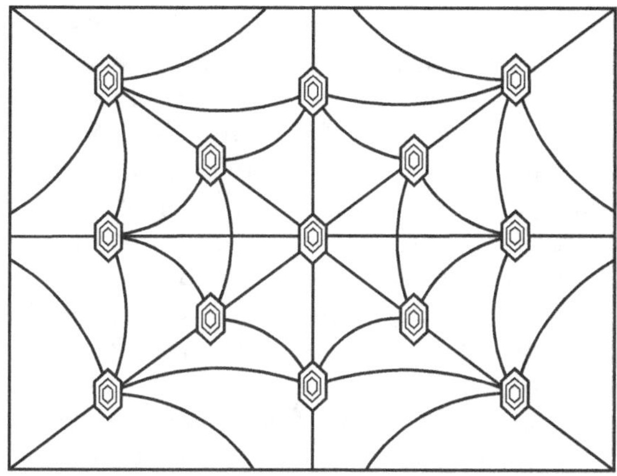

imus at some point in their lives to achieve individuation with the help of another. Ultimately, as one grooves into one's own way of flourishing, as complemented by paying attention to the unique needs of the flourishing of other living entities, one becomes closer to achieving *ming*, the ability to serve as a mirror to the various *de* as they are spontaneously (*ziran*) found in their interdependent relations as mediated by one's own being. The Velvet Underground song "I'll Be Your Mirror" is a fitting description of this mirroring at the level of person to person.

Put together, the earth in Daoism comes to reveal itself as a vast interrelated network of *de* mirroring each other in their own unique ways. After my journey to China, I began my master's work under the guidance of Kwang-Sae Lee, who explained the Daoist worldview with the most famous metaphor utilized by Fazang in the Huayan school of Chinese Buddhism—namely, the jewel net of Indra. That metaphor depicts a vast net with a jewel at each intersection or nexus, such that each jewel reflects all other jewels, symbolizing the universe as a complex and intricate web of interdependent relationships. As a unique individual, you are meant to shine like a jewel, and so is every other living being in their own unique ways. If you are in a rut right now or addicted to an entity that is not serving you, know that this is not your proper nature. Any flourishing, if it is to be sustained, must be aligned with what is ultimately natural or proper. Humans especially are meant to shine brightly, given their highly complex brain structure that we discussed in the last chapter. Alan Watts helps us to visualize Indra's net by imaging a multidimensional spider's web early in the morning covered with drops of dew. Every single dew drop contains the reflection of all other dew drops, and those reflections contain the reflections of all other dew drops in that reflection.

The book of *Zhuangzi* is helpful in understanding how variegated human versions of shining can be. Unlike Laozi, who was almost certainly not a historical person, Zhuangzi probably was a real person, and his book comprises the "inner chapters," written by Zhuangzi himself, and the "outer chapters," written by later thinkers who engaged with his ideas. In it, we meet eclectic figures who become extremely adept at artisanal crafts like carving bell stands or wheels by following the natural curvature of the wood, catching cicadas by following their natural movements, butchering animals by following their natural anatomy, or swimming in treacherous waters gracefully by moving effortlessly with the natural flow. Zhuangzi can help us to see that human flourishing happens in a plethora of ways, as long as we cultivate what the Daoists call *wuwei*—masterful but effortless "action" that accords with the *dao*.

Recent research in positive psychology by Mihaly Csiksezentmihalyi and others has shown that being in flow—that is, being in a state of complete absorption in an activity that one loves and is working to master—is a critical aspect of human flourishing. Anyone who has mastered a musical instrument knows this, as do athletes who regularly get into flow. Video games are a common means for persons to experience this state. In order for all of us to flourish in our own unique ways, we need to accord with the natural unfolding of things, what in my own experience I understand as the *dao*. As the book of Zhuangzi informs us, though, when the world has lost the *dao*, the *dao* has lost the world. Just as *yin* and *yang* complement each other as life forces, *de* and *dao* serve as complementary in terms of focus and field. Discovering your unique way of thriving is your purpose in life, and you will know when you have found it. You need to keep in mind, though, that your flourishing is contingent upon the earth system staying within the parameters outlined above. We all have work to do to heal that system in order to provide ourselves the conditions to flourish in our own unique ways.

This truth leads us to the last step of our journey together, which is Confucianism. Like many spiritual leaders, Kongzi outlines the stages he went through in terms of learning and self-discovery. At the age of fifteen he set himself on a path of learning, at thirty he began to establish himself in the world, a task most of us do at a professional and a personal level, at forty he started to gain wisdom and clarity as to the nature of his self, at fifty he gained a greater sense of his relationship with the cosmic order, at sixty he became more attuned to others, and at seventy he fully aligned himself with the *dao*. I've found that the actual age markers aren't as important as the stages themselves, as I have met some persons who have cultivated a life of wisdom in my own life. It is clearly the case that some find their place earlier than others. You are currently at a certain life stage and it is absolutely crucial that you prioritize yourself and begin to understand how you groove into the broader picture of the world, which lies at the heart of the human-nature relationship, the very subject we've been exploring. For Kongzi, the change absolutely must begin with the individual, a sentiment Jung shared as well. Once one can come to terms with who one is, embracing both the darker and the brighter aspects of the self, one can begin to live in one's own truth. That very sincerity leads to a rectification of the *xin*, that is, the heart-mind (the Chinese don't separate reason and emotions as clearly as thinkers in most Western traditions); in this process of rectification, one can achieve sincerity in thought, which will then mold a virtuous character. The individual then shares this knowledge first with one's family, then with one's friends, and eventually with one's community and the state more broadly, with the ultimate extension of this ripple effect changing the entirety of the world. In 1913, Mahatma Gandhi stated plainly that "if we could change ourselves, the tendencies in the world would also change." That is the heart of the matter.

All of this may sound outlandish but, given our current state of the world in terms of politics and corporate power dynamics, there is simply no other way. Change must come from the bottom up. For the Confucians, two vital rules need to be heeded in order for all of this to function as it ought. First, we need to heed the doctrine of the rectification of names (*zhengming*), in which we call things by their rightful names so that we can gain clarity into the truth. We've seen how the ultra-wealthy have utilized propaganda tactics to divert us from the truth, but Kongzi knew that it is in our nature to see through them. Misinformation and disinformation are very real infodemics that you and I can help to curb. Second, we need to call people out who are exploiting others for their own mere personal benefit. Kant was right that all humans are autonomous, meaning we have the right to live our lives in accordance with our own version of flourishing as long as that flourishing does not negatively affect the flourishing of others. Kongzi understood this as well and insists that leaders in particular be held accountable to the truth. To ensure a social order that aligns with the ultimate order of the universe, the "mandate of heaven" (*tianming*) prescribes the removal of leaders who are not in accord with reality and bend the truth to their own merely personal interests, thus not serving as proper leaders (*tian* is typically translated as "heaven" but really means the supreme force that governs the universe, including the trajectory of human affairs). True leadership is selfless in nature, as Laozi informs us throughout the *Daodejing*. Newer leadership styles that align with servant leadership echo this truth from the past. It is not as if Confucianism or Daoism are the only ways; they are simply the ones I have found salient. The question is what you are drawn toward; follow the truth and it will set you free.

We've come a long way together. Whether anything I've said is true is really a matter of your own discretion. I do believe if we are going to change things back toward the truth and right the civilizational ship, we need to shift our priorities. We already celebrate greatness in so many different ways. Our towering musical artists are met with the adoration of crowds due to their ability to shine creatively with the help of their right brains, since that is a trait that is not cultivated by many of us in left-hemispheric dominant societies. Bands like the Beatles took the world by storm in the 1960s with their ability to jive together. It is reported that Metallica played in front of 1.5 million fans in Moscow in 1991, thus showcasing the attraction of a band that is willing to engage with the darker sides of human nature in a positive way. There is undeniable power in music. The same attraction occurs in sports. We know that play is related to the limbic system, and those who are able to master a sport are met with nearly universal praise, likely also because of our left-hemispheric dominance and its craving for integration of the darker aspects of the brain. Michael Jordan, who, to my mind, is the greatest basketball player ever, has created an entire logo behind his iconic "Jumpman" image based on a photo taken by a person, as it happens, with my family name, Jacobus "Co" Willem Rentmeester. It is fitting that Co's image was created in preparation for the 1984 Olympics, in which Jordan was ready to take off on a world stage. This human-nature narrative, if it is to take off, will also require a logo. I suggest that the peace symbol serves that purpose.

This image was born of a place of love in 1958 as a symbol for nuclear disarmament and thus world peace. For our purposes, the line down the middle symbolizes the biosphere, the two angles signify the hydrosphere and the geosphere, and the circle signifies the atmosphere. You, as a brilliant human being, are smack dab in the middle of these spheres and ultimately must help to determine the trajectory of the world. Those who can express greatness and shine the brightest through enacting the entirety of their brains, thereby showcasing colossal wisdom—*colossophia*, as we have come to call it—ought to be celebrated above all. The Dalai Lama currently shines brightly in this regard, as his life has been dedicated to peace and harmony for all sentient beings. Mahatma Gandhi was no different, and neither are you and I. In attempting to heal Gaia, we will not only imbue meaning into our lives but also provide that opportunity to others. The time to do so, however, is closing fast. We must create a movement that sweeps the world, and it all begins with standing in the truth.

We've only just begun this journey, but we must end this narrative for now, as the main pieces of the puzzle have

been laid bare. One must stop somewhere, as Aristotle informs us in the *Metaphysics*. It is only fitting to end this narrative with the words of Bob Dylan, who recognized that the times were a-changin' during the countercultural revolution of the 1960s. In "All Along the Watchtower" he sings, "So let us not talk falsely now; the hour's getting late." Not ten but a mere four years after that space in time when the hippie dream of peace and love was fading away, Alvin Lee sang, "I'd love to change the world / But I don't know what to do / So I'll leave it up to you." We now know what to do. We need to share this story and save human civilizations as we have come to know them by enacting a countercultural revolution. May the odds be ever in our favor.

Afterword

This manifesto was written on the heels of profound suffering in both my personal and professional life. On November 1, 2024, a simple act of kindness opened my eyes to the beauty of life, thus shifting my own perspective away from the destructive nihilism that had overtaken me. Through my mentors and the philosophers and spiritual leaders who have informed this work, as coupled by the increasingly clear scientific understanding of the planet system, it has become evident that we need nothing less than a radical shift in our understanding of the human place on the planet. I've tried to show that the first shift is to move away from the merely rational *persona* (mask) and toward the more wholly integrated rational animal. The second shift is to understand our proper relationship with Gaia as intrinsically interconnected with all living beings. Heidegger understood some of this in his notion of *Geviert*, the fourfold, which is his name for the interconnection between the earth, sky, mortals, and gods. For us, the fourfold connects the human as an instantiation of the biosphere, which is connected to the geosphere and hydrosphere and inextricably encompassed by the atmosphere. This connection must be respected as sacred. In Heidegger's *Contributions to Philosophy*, we come to see that, as Richard Polt so helpfully informs us, a genuine encounter with the world—"the earth on which we dwell, the tools we use, the art we create, the communities in which we try to work out our goals"—requires a mutual emerging of our own unfolding and a receptivity toward the significance of beings as a whole. Any philosopher or spiritual leader who still respects the truth recognizes that an alignment with the truth requires both self-emergence and receptivity from the very place in which you stand here and now. Through Jung and Stevens, we now know that this is a matter of connecting the logical, analytical left-hemispheric functions with the intuitive, synthetic functions of the right hemisphere of the brain to become whole.

In reality, this happens at both the individual and the cultural level. Jung once pointed to the Iron Curtain, the Berlin Wall, as a symbolic representation of the separation between the East and the West, the dark and the light. That wall fell in 1989 when I was merely six years old, but the East and West are still separated culturally even if corporate capitalism has swept nearly the entire globe. It is time for you and me to bring the two together and stand up by creating a more culturally connected world that is not based on the mere callous cash payment–based relationships that Karl Marx and Friedrich Engels rightfully critiqued, and we can look to an ancient myth to help us in doing so. In various schools of Daoism and Confucianism, they utilize the myth of the *fenghuang* as a symbol of harmony and world peace. The immortal bird combines both male and female elements to form a *yang* and *yin* harmony, the *animus* and the *anima*, if you prefer Jung's language. Legend has it that the appearance of the bird in a dream signifies a shift toward peaceful rule that enables prosperity. In order to awaken *fenghuang* symbolically, we need to embody the *wu de*, the five Confucian virtues that have been passed down from generation to generation in China, our longest-standing civilization on earth. We must, as Kongzi understood, learn from the past, a lesson your grandparents have probably tried to pass down to you. These virtues are *ren* (benevolence), *yi* (righteousness), *li* (propriety), *zhi* (wisdom), and *xin* (integrity).

Mengzi, the person responsible for popularizing Confucianism, understood humans to have *siduan*, four incipient tendencies of the *xin* (heart-mind) to align with these. Compassion is the feeling of distress at others' suffering, and its cultivation leads to *ren*, benevolence, or, better yet, *humaneness*. Shame and disgust are the feelings that are invoked when one encounters wrong actions, whether in oneself or in that of another, and promote a sense of *yi*, righteousness or justice. Deference and respect for others provides a sense of modesty that encourages a respect for *li*, propriety or proper social etiquette. Our intuitive sense of right and wrong cultivates *zhi*, wisdom in which we are capable of accurate moral discernment. When all of these incipient tendencies are properly formed, we achieve *xin*, integrity, and thus become whole. Aristotle's word for that was *eudaimonia*, a good life. Mengzi appropriately compares these tendencies to seeds or sprouts since they are naturally present in the human being; they simply need the appropriate conditions to flourish.

If you are skeptical about whether human nature is inherently good or inherently bad, Mengzi can help us to see that humans are capable of both horrifying atrocities, as perpetrated and witnessed in Nazi Germany, but also profound kindness that has been witnessed all across the world, from Mother Teresa's selfless work in Calcutta to care for the poorest of the poor to Thich Nhat Hanh's work in Vietnam, which spread the principles of nonviolence, compassion, and solidarity throughout the world. We do not necessarily have to point to extremes. Every single one of us has witnessed the power of human connection and kindness at some point in our lives. In the Confucian tradition, Mengzi provides the example of a child about to fall into a well.

Unless a human being is completely perverted from their incipient tendency of compassion and thus "too far gone," the individual will naturally feel the need to help the child and steer it away from danger. That is because *humans, at our core, are empathetic beings capable of protecting one another, even strangers.* This is why the proper word for human in China is *ren*, humaneness.

How pure are you in your *xin* (heart-mind)? Put in another way, how much integrity do you have? You have *ren* built into you by evolutionary design, but have you cultivated humaneness fully yet? Aristotle was right that the only way to cultivate these virtues is by putting yourself in situations that call for them. Are you doing this on a regular basis? What of *yi*? Have you taken a stand for social justice? The world is literally dying for you to wake up and take your proper stand, as are the countless persons suffering around you. It doesn't take a Martin Luther King Jr. or a Malala Yousafzai to do this; it takes you and me, here and now. If you see injustice in your local community, stand up to it, since humans are meant to flourish. If we don't, we will get more of the same, which in the current context means ultra-wealthy cruising in giga-yachts while you and I continue to engage in mere shadowboxing as we bandy about the *doxes*, the mere opinions often propagated by the very masters of humankind themselves.

Li, social etiquette, is more important in the East than it is in the West simply because much of the West has succumbed to what Charles Taylor has called self-centered individualism that can decay into self-absorption and moral relativism, two traits that are insidiously damaging to any sense of true community. And yet, there are still some sacred social rituals in the West, as anyone who has been to a military funeral understands at an experiential level. What would it mean for you to engage in social etiquette that honored your audience rather than merely honored yourself? Social media influencers should take this question to heart.

And finally, what of *zhe*, wisdom? How much of your time is spent learning from those who came before you and those who are among you that are wiser in the ways of the world than you? When is the last time you called an elder relative and asked about the meaning of life from that person's perspective? Some of you prioritize your bodily physique and have become beautiful because of it. Are you also capable of prioritizing your soul? How much of your time is spent distracted away from your true self through media, consumeristic tendencies, or addictive behaviors? What if you could take a little of that time and shift your priority, just a smidge, toward the cultivation of wisdom. This is not a matter of giving up your streaming platforms, social media accounts, gaming devices, shopping habits, alcohol or whatever other substances you prefer to help you unwind; after all, even Socrates enjoyed a good drink. Rather, it is a matter of complementing your leisure with wisdom work, thereby cultivating *phronesis*, practical wisdom, by integrating philosophy and the humanities more broadly or the arts, or, of course, religion, depending upon what you are drawn toward. It is a matter of cultivating colossal wisdom that integrates the left and right hemispheres of your brain through yoga, meditation, or learning a musical instrument or a new language; it could be practicing an Eastern martial art not for war but for self-growth, or any other activity that combines the logical aspects of yourself with the creative ones. That sweet spot—the connection between rationality and animality as physically situated in the corpus callosum—shines in unique ways depending on the individual. If we can awaken our whole selves and achieve *xin*, integrity, and have the courage to share ourselves with the world, we can't help but awaken *fenghuang* on a more collective level.

If your unique way of shining operates in accordance with the global parameters of sustainability that we outlined in the last chapter and you have the courage to shine brightly, you will help to right the civilizational ship.

Your transcendence, or *ex*-istence, that is, your unique way of standing out, must begin from where you are. My own trajectory can't help but have been informed by my home state, Wisconsin, whose motto is "Forward." Like every other state, Wisconsin has produced brilliant people, including naturalists like Aldo Leopold and John Muir (who was not born there but called it home since the age of eleven), artists like Bon Iver and the Violent Femmes, the architect Frank Lloyd Wright, and others. Each flourished because they were able to be their unique selves and cultivate virtues that accorded with their own unique talents. It is time for you and me to do the same. Shining brightly in your own unique way that respects the flourishing of others within ecosystemic parameters is the recipe for saving human civilizations as we have come to know them. This is what it means to breathe life back into the rational animal. We all must channel our inner Tupac, a fellow American whose life was cut too short, in order to do so: "It's time for us as a people to start makin' some changes / Let's change the way we eat / Let's change the way we live / And let's change the way we treat each other / You see, the old way wasn't workin' / So it's on us to do what we gotta do to survive." Therein lies colossal wisdom. Godspeed in your trajectory forward.

Cast of Characters

Gerhard Adler
(1904–1988) British psychologist

Ahura Mazda
God (Zoroastrianism)

Al–Hallaj
(858–922) Islamic poet

Albertus Magnus
(ca. 1193–1280) German Dominican friar

Allah
God (Islam)

Roger Ames
(1947–present) Canadian–born philosopher

Thomas Aquinas
(ca. 1221–1274) Combined Aristotle and Christianity

Aristotle
(ca. 384–322 BCE) Greek polymath

Augustine of Hippo
(c. 354–430) Combined Plato and Christianity

Marcus Aurelius
(121–180) Stoic Roman Emperor

James H. Austin
(1925–present) American neurologist

Francis Bacon
(1561–1626) English empiricist

James Mark Baldwin
(1861–1934) American psychologist

Roland Barthes
(1915–1980) French philosopher

The Beatles
(1960–1970) British band

Edward Bernays
(1891–1995) Austrian–American propaganda pioneer

Ludwig von Bertalanffy
(1901–1972) Austrian biologist

Ludwig Binswanger
(1881–1966) Swiss psychiatrist

Eugen Bleuler
(1857–1939) Swiss psychiatrist

Gustav Krupp von Bohlen und Halbach
(1870–1950) German industrialist

Bon Iver
(2006–present) American band

Medard Boss
(1903–1990) Swiss psychoanalyst

John Bowlby
(1907–1990) British psychiatrist

Franz Brentano
(1838–1917) German philosopher and psychologist

Julius Caeser
(100–44 BCE) First Roman emperor

Albert Camus
(1913–1960) French philosopher

Irene Champernowne
(1901–1976) British art therapist

Pierre Teilhard de Chardin
(1881–1955) French Catholic priest

Coldplay
(1996–present) English band

Colossal Biosciences
(2021–present) American biotechnology company

Constantine
(272–337) Christian Roman emperor

Erik Conway
(1965–present) American historian

Nicolaus Copernicus
(1473–1543) Polish polymath

Paul Crutzen
(1933–2021) Dutch atmospheric chemist

Mihaly Csiksezentmihalyi
(1934–2021) Hungarian–American psychologist

Dalai Llama
(1935–present) Spiritual leader of Tibetan Buddhism

Charles Darwin
(1809–1882) Founder of evolutionary biology

Richard Davidson
(1951–present) American psychologist

Guy Debord
(1931–1994) French philosopher/situationist

René Descartes
(1596–1650) French rationalist

Jennifer Doudna
(1964–present) American biochemist

Hubert Dreyfus
(1929–2017) American philosopher

Eugène Dubois
(1858–1940) Dutch paleoanthropologist

William Durham
(1949–present) American biological anthropologist

Bob Dylan
(1941–present) American musician

Meister Eckhart
(ca. 1260–1328) German Catholic priest

Ralph Waldo Emerson
(1803–1882) American transcendentalist

Friedrich Engels
(1820–1895) German philosopher

Epictetus
(ca. 55–135) Stoic philosopher

Explosions in the Sky
(1999–present) American band

Hans Eysenck
(1916–1997) German-British psychologist

Fazang
(643–712) Chinese Buddhist (Huayan School)

Francis of Assisi
(1182–1226) Founder of Franciscan Order

Marie-Louise von Franz
(1915–1998) Jungian analyst

Sigmund Freud
(1856–1939) Founder of psychoanalysis

Erich Fromm
(1900–1980) German social psychologist

Gaia
Earth as a system

Mahatma Gandhi
(1869–1948) Indian spiritual leader

Siddhartha Gautama
(ca. 563–ca. 483 BCE) Founder of Buddhism

Joseph Goebbels
(1897–1945) German propagandist

Charles Guignon
(1944–2020) American
philosopher

Ernst Haeckel
(1834–1919) German
naturalist

David Hall
(1937–2001) American
philosopher

James Hansen
(1941–present) American
climatologist

**Eduard von
Hartmann**
(1842–1906) German
philosopher

He Jiankui
(1984–present) Chinese
biophysicist

Johann Peter Hebel
(1760–1826) German
poet

G. W. F. Hegel
(1770–1831) German
idealist

Martin Heidegger
(1889–1976) German
philosopher

Joseph Henderson
(1903–2007) American
Jungian psychologist

Heraclitus
(ca. 535–ca. 475 BCE)
Presocratic philosopher

Adolf Hitler
(1889–1945) German
politician

George Hogenson
(1927–2021) American
psychologist

Friedrich Hölderlin
(1770–1843) German
poet

Gerald Holton
(1922–present) American historian of science

Andrew Huberman
(1975–present) American
neuroscientist

David Hume
(1711–1776) British empiricist

Edmund Husserl
(1859–1938) Founder of phenomenology

Ibn Arabi
(1165–1240) Islamic poet

Ibn Rushd/Averroes
(ca. 1122–1198) Islamic polymath

Ibn Sina/Avicenna
(ca. 980–1037) Islamic polymath

Indra
Hindu deity

Karl Jaspers
(1883–1969) German-Swiss philosopher/theologian

Peter Jeanmaire
(1935–present) German physicist

Jesus of Nazareth
(ca. 1–30/33) God incarnate (Christianity)

Michael Jordan
(1963–present) American athlete

Carl Jung
(1875–1961) Founder of analytical psychology

Immanuel Kant
(1724–1804) German polymath

Sean Kelly
(1967–present) American philosopher

King Gizzard & the Lizard Wizard
(2010–present) Australian band

Martin Luther King Jr.
(1929–1968) American Baptist minister

Elizabeth Kolbert
(1961–present) American journalist

Kongzi
(551–479 BCE) Founder of Confucianism

Conradin Kreutzer
(1780–1849) German composer

Laozi
"Founder" of Daoism

Led Zeppelin
(1968–1980) British band

Alvin Lee
(1944–2013) English musician

Kwang-Sae Lee
(1934–2012) Korean-American philosopher

Gottfried Wilhelm Leibniz
(1646–1716) German polymath

Aldo Leopold
(1887–1948) American naturalist

Max Lerner
(1902–1992) American educator

John Locke
(1632–1704) British empiricist

Konrad Lorenz
(1903–1989) Austrian ethologist

Louis XVI
(1754–1793) Last King of France

James Lovelock
(1919–2022) Founder of Gaia theory

Amory Lovins
(1947–present) American physicist

Eileen Luders
(1977–present) German neuroscientist

The Lumineers
(2005–present) American band

Alexander Luria
(1902–1977) Russian neuropsychogist

Isaac Luria
(1534–1572) Jewish rabbi

Niccolo Machiavelli
(1469–1527) Italian political realist

Paul MacLean
(1913–2007) American neuroscientist

Bob Marley
(1945–1981) Jamaican reggae musician

Karl Marx
(1818–1883) German philosopher/revolutionary

Iain McGilchrist
(1953–present) British psychiatrist

Mengzi
(372–289 BCE) Confucian philosopher

Metallica
(1981–present) American band

Moses
Hebrew prophet

Moses de León
(1240–1305) Spanish rabbi

Mother Teresa
(1910–1997) Indian Catholic nun

Muhammad
(ca. 570–632) Islamic seal of the prophets

John Muir
(1838–1914) American naturalist

Jacob Needleman
(1934–2022) American philosopher

Isaac Newton
(1643–1727) English polymath

Thich Nhat Hanh
(1926–2022) Vietnamese Buddhist monk

Nicomachus
Aristotle's father

Friedrich Nietzsche
(1844–1900) German philosopher

Niggaz Wit Attitudes (N.W.A.)
(1987–1991) American band

Nirvana
(1987–1994) American band

Keiji Nishitani
(1900–1990) Japanese philosopher

Ochwiay Biano
(1885–1976) Elder of Taos Pueblo

William of Ockham
(ca. 1288–1348) Franciscan friar

Naomi Oreskes
(1958–present) American historian of science

Robert Ornstein
(1942–present) American psychologist

Evan Osnos
(1976–present) American journalist

Paul
(ca. 5–64/65) Popularized Christianity

Corine Pelluchon
(1967–present) French philosopher

Tom Petty
(1950–2017) American musician

Plato
(ca. 427–347 BCE) Founded the Academy

Richard Polt
(1964–present) American philosopher

Protagoras
(ca. 481–420 BCE) Sophist

Rabia al–Adawiyya
(713–801) Islamic poet

Rage Against the Machine
(1991–present) American band

Raphael
(1483–1520) Italian Renaissance artist

Lou Reed
(1942–2013) American musician

Jacobus Willem Rentmeester
(1936–present) Dutch photojournalist

William Richardson
(1920–2016) American philosopher

Johan Rockström
(1965–present) Swedish scientist

The Rolling Stones
(1962–present) English band

Edgar Rubin
(1886–1951) Danish psychologist

F. W. J. von Schelling
(1775–1854) German idealist

Martin Schönfeld
(1963–2020) German-American philosopher

Arthur Schopenhauer
(1788–1860) German pessimist

Seneca the Younger
(ca. 4 BCE–65 CE) Stoic Roman statesman

B. F. Skinner
(1904–1990) American psychologist

Adam Smith
(1723–1790) Founder of modern economics

Socrates
(ca. 469–399 BCE) Paradigmatic philosopher

Roger Sperry
(1913–1994) American neuroscientist

Speusippus
(ca. 408–339 BCE)
Plato's nephew

Baruch Spinoza
(1632–1677) Dutch rationalist

Anthony Stevens
(1933–2023) British psychiatrist

Charles Taylor
(1931–present) Canadian philosopher

Thales
(ca. 624–546 BCE) First known Western philosopher

Henry David Thoreau
(1817–1862) American transcendentalist

Greta Thunberg
(2003–present) Swedish climate activist

Fritz Thyssen
(1873–1951) German businessman

Nikolaas Tinbergen
(1907–1988) Dutch biologist

Tool
(1990–present) American band

Tupac Shakur
(1971–1996) American musician

The Velvet Underground
(1964–1973) American band

Violent Femmes
(1980–present) American band

Alan Watts
(1915–1973) British philosopher

Lynn White Jr.
(1907–1987) American historian

Richard Wilhelm
(1873–1930) German sinologist

E. O. Wilson
(1929–2021) American biologist

Christian Wolff
(1679–1754) German rationalist

Frank Lloyd Wright
(1867–1959) American architect

Yahweh
God (Judaism)

You
(–present)
To be determined

Malala Yousafzai
(1997–present) Pakistani female education activist

Zarathustra/ Zoroaster
Founder of Zoroastrianism

Zhuangzi
(ca. 369–ca. 286 BCE) Daoist philosopher

GLOSSARY

Absoluter Geist	Absolute Spirit, the ultimate reality (Hegel)
abyss	the dark, creative power of mother earth (Hölderlin)
the Academy	The first known university in the Western world founded by Plato
ACT (American College Test)	standardized test used for college admissions in the United States
aether	the father of light (Hölderlin)
Ahriman	dark and evil force (Zoroastrianism)
algorithmic suggestion	a personalized suggestion for content, products, or services based on consumer preferences (a.k.a. algorithmic recommendation)
American Disenlightenment	an age marked by anti-intellectualism, authoritarian tendencies, and the devaluation of the humanities (Schönfeld)

Apollo — Greek god of light and truth

anatman — no-self (Buddhism)

anima — spirit, breath, soul (Latin)

anima — the unconscious feminine archetype within a man's psyche (Jung)

anima mundi — the world soul (Latin)

animus — the unconscious masculine archetype within a woman's psyche (Jung)

the Anthropocene — the current era in which human influence on the planet has geological significance (Crutzen)

anthropocentrism — the view that human beings are the center of the universe

anthropogenic climate change — climate change that is the result of human activity

anthropos — human being (Greek)

antithesis — that which negates (Hegel)

apaideusia — the uneducated (Greek)

archetype — inherited, fundamental pattern of thought or behavior that shapes human experience (Jung)

archetypal symbol-ism	universal, recurring symbols or patterns across cultures that represent fundamental human experiences or emotions
arete	virtue, excellent trait (Greek)
ataraxia	mental tranquility (Stoicism)
atmos	gas, vapor (Greek)
atmosphere	earth system domain consisting of air
attachment theory	a psychological framework that examines emotional bonds that form through relationships, especially between infants and their caregivers (Bowlby)
attention-deficit/hyperactivity disorder (ADHD)	a mental condition characterized by persistent difficulty in maintaining attention
attractor	the state toward which a system tends toward over time
Aufklärung	enlightenment (Kant)
atman	soul (Hinduism)

the Axial Age a period from roughly the 8th to 3rd century BCE that experienced significant shifts philosophically and religiously (Karl Jaspers)

"back to the things themselves" motto of phenomenology (Husserl)

the Baldwin effect a proposed evolutionary mechanism in which learned behaviors influence genetic evolution (Baldwin)

beatitudo highest form of happiness (Aquinas)

behaviorism a school of psychology that emphasizes the study of observable behavior and how it is learned through interactions with one's environment

Berlin Wall the wall separating West Berlin from East Berlin from 1961 to 1989, a symbolic representation of the separation between the West and the East

besinnliches Denken meditative thinking (Heidegger)

besinnungslos thoughtless, senseless, unconscious (Heidegger)

Bessinungslosigkeit	thoughtlessness (Heidegger)
Bestand	a repository of mere resources on hand to be maximally exploited (Heidegger)
Bhavagad Gita	Hindu sacred text
Bildung	education, formation, enculturation (German)
biogenetic law	the theory that evolutionary stages are repeated in the growth of a young animal
bios	life (Greek)
biosphere	earth system domain consisting of life
biosphere integrity	the health and functionality of the earth's living systems
bipolarity	the state of having two extremes, implying opposing yet complementary forces
the Black Death	the bubonic plague
boulesis	rational desire (Greek)
Brahman	the ultimate reality (Hinduism)

Buddha   "awakened one" ("the Buddha" refers specifically to Siddhartha Gautama)

calculus   a branch of mathematics focused on the study of the change of matter in motion broken down into differential calculus (dealing with rates of change) and integral calculus (dealing with accumulation)

carbon dioxide   a colorless, odorless gas produced by burning organic compounds, the element carbon, and respiration

Cartesian coordinates   a two-dimensional grid system that enables one to define the position of points in a plane or space (geometry)

cerebral imperialism   the process of the dominant hemispheric brain functioning overshadowing the other hemisphere's functioning (Stevens)

Christ   the Anointed One (Greek)

circulatory system   the system of organs and blood vessels that circulate blood throughout the body

climate — weather conditions prevailing in general over a long period of time

climate change — long-term shifts in temperatures and weather patterns

climate refugee — a person who has been forced to leave his or her home as a result of the effects of climate change

closed system — a system that does not exchange matter with its surroundings but only exchanges energy

cogito ergo sum — "I think, therefore, I am" (Descartes)

the collective unconscious — the shared, inherited layer of the unconscious mind common to all of humanity (Jung)

colossal thinking — thinking that integrates the left hemisphere with the right hemisphere

colossal wisdom (colossophia) — wisdom that integrates the left hemisphere with the right hemisphere, thereby informing practice

complex a pattern of unconscious, emotionally charged thoughts, feelings, memories, and perceptions organized around a central theme that influences behavior (Jung)

conscious mind the part of the mind that contains thoughts, feelings, and memories of which we are currently aware (Freud)

consumerism cultural phenomenon where spending on goods or services is tied to human happiness

contemptus mundi a contempt for the material world (Latin, especially Aquinas)

Copernican revolution the claim that objects must conform to human knowledge, rather than the other way around (Kant)

corporate capitalism a form of capitalism characterized by the dominance of large corporations that control the means of production to generate profit

corpus callosum a band of nerve fibers joining the two hemispheres of the brain

Council	formal gathering of leaders (Christianity)
CRISPR-Cas9	a gene-editing technology that can cut DNA at a desired location
crux immissa quadrata	the cross with four equal lengths used in early Christianity
daimon	spirit, transcendent guiding force (Greek)
dao	the way of nature (ancient China)
Daodejing	the book of *dao* and *de* (Daoism)
Dasein	human existence (Heidegger)
de	virtue; efficacy (Daoism)
de-extinction	the process of bringing back an extinct species
deforestation	the clearing of trees
Denken	thinking (German)
Deus sive Natura	God as Nature (Spinoza)
dialectic	natural processual unfolding of an idea from thesis to antithesis to synthesis (Hegel)
dialogue	inquiry that operates through logos

Dionysus	Greek god of wine, fertility, and ecstasy
direct-to-consumer pharmaceutical advertising	the marketing of prescription drugs directly to the consumer
disinformation	misinformation intended to mislead its audience
DNA	a self-replicating material in all living beings that functions as the carrier of genetic information
doxa (plural: doxes)	mere opinion (Greek)
ecocrisis	a state of environmental degradation so wide-ranging that it threatens the perpetuation of the human species
ego	the part of the psyche that mediates between the id, superego, and the external world (Freud)
eidos	outward look, form (Plato)
Eigentlichkeit	the mode of being in which the human has owned one's own unique existence (Heidegger)
Elohim	gods (pre-monotheistic Judaism)

embryology	the branch of biology that studies the development of embryos
emerging (emergent) systems theory	a framework that examines how complex systems exhibit novel properties and behaviors that are not apparent in the individual components alone
empiricism	The philosophical doctrine that knowledge primarily originates from sensory experience
the Enlightenment	intellectual movement in the 17th and 18th centuries that sought to improve society through reasoned inquiry
entelechy	matter in a state of perceptively striving toward it proper end (Leibniz)
epithumia	bodily pleasure (Greek)
Erde	earth as a dark, creative force (Heidegger)
ergon	work, action (Greek)
eros	desire, love (especially in the passionate or sexual sense) (Greek)

ethos — character, habit, custom, cultural milieu (Greek)

euangelion — "good news" (Greek)

eudaimonia — living well; good life (Greek)

feedback loop — a process where the output of a system is returned as input, creating a cycle

feeling — an emotion or affective belief (psychology)

fenghuang — mythical Chinese bird sometimes understood as "the Chinese phoenix" that represents peace, harmony, and the union of yin and yang

fertilizer — a chemical or natural substance added to soil to increase its fertility (e.g., nitrogen, phosphorus)

finis — end, purpose (Latin)

flow — a state in which a person is fully immersed and deeply engaged in an activity (positive psychology)

fossil fuels — a natural fuel formed in the geosphere from the remains of living organisms

French Revolution — period of radical sociopolitical change in France in which the monarchy was overthrown

frontier mentality — the mindset that the frontier, the wild, is meant to be conquered or mastered by humans

Führer — leader (Nazi)

Führerbunker — underground complex that served as Nazi headquarters

Führerprinzip — The doctrine that the Führer held absolute authority, thus entailing that all levels of government must align with the Führer's vision (Nazi)

Gaia — earth as a living system (Lovelock)

Gestell — the frame of reality as a totality of resources to align with human interests (Heidegger)

das Gegenständige — the universe understood as objects standing against a subject (Heidegger)

Geist — spirit, will (Hegel)

general systems theory (GST)   an interdisciplinary framework that studies how systems, both natural and social, are organized and function

generative artificial intelligence (AI)   technology that creates content based on learned patterns from existing data

genoi hoios essi mathon   become what you are (Greek)

geo   earth (Greek), the ground

geoengineering   technologies aimed at intentionally manipulating the Earth's climate (e.g., solar radiation management, carbon dioxide removal)

geosphere   earth system domain consisting of solid matter

Gestalt shift   when one's interpretation of an experience changes from one frame to another; a sudden perceptual change

global capitalism   the economic system characterized by the worldwide exchange of goods, services, and capital

gigayacht   a superyacht exceeding 100 yards (90 meters) in length

gnothi seauton	know thyself (Greek)
Gospels	stories of God (Christianity)
the Great Pacific Garbage Patch	a conglomeration of trillions of pieces of plastic in the Pacific Ocean
greenhouse gases	atmospheric gases that absorb and emit radiant energy, trapping heat in the earth's atmosphere
he	harmony (Daoism)
das Heilige	the holy (Hölderlin)
hero	archetype that represents the embodiment of courage, strength, and often integrates the journey towards self-discovery (Jung)
hesed	loving-kindness (Judaism)
Holy Spirit	active presence of God in the world (Christianity)
Homo erectus	the first species to evolve a humanlike body and gait and discover how to build a fire
Homo sapiens	humans regarded as a species, literally "wise human" in Latin
hule	matter (Greek)

human immunodeficiency virus (HIV)	a virus that attacks the body's immune system
Hume's guillotine	the thesis that you cannot derive a prescriptive (ought) claim from a descriptive (is) claim (a.k.a. the is-ought "problem")
hupokeimenon	subject, that which lies beneath (Greek)
hydraulic fracturing	the injection of water, sand, and chemicals at high pressure to enhance the extraction of oil or natural gas, a.k.a. "fracking"
hydro	water (Greek)
hydrosphere	earth system domain consisting of water
hyperconsumerism	the excessive consumption of goods and services that far exceed basic human needs or functionality
hypoxic zone	an area with low oxygen levels (*hypo* means "under" and *oxic* refers to oxygen), a dead zone
id	the most primitive part of the human psyche driven by the pleasure principle and focused on immediate gratification of eros, desire (Freud)

idea

form, intellectual blueprint (Plato)

imago Dei

image or likeness of God (Latin)

imprinting

a rapid, irreversible form of learning where a young animal forms a strong attachment to the first moving object it encounters (Lorenz)

In-der-Welt-Sein

being-in-the-world (Heidegger)

incarnate word

divine logos (Christianity)

individuation

a process of psychological integration wherein a person develops a unique sense of self by integrating conscious and unconscious aspects of their personality (Jung)

Industrial Revolution

a period of major technological advancement that transformed energy production processes toward fossil-fuel based systems

infodemic

literally "information upon the people"

Inshallah

actions that align with the will of Allah (Islam)

instinct — an innate, typically fixed pattern of behavior in response to stimuli (biology)

interhemispheric transfer — the process of transferring information between the two cerebral hemispheres of the brain

Interpretatio Romana — Roman interpretation of Greek deities

intuition — a way of perceiving the world that relies on unconscious processes (psychology)

the Ionian Enchantment — the belief that the natural world is fundamentally orderly that began in the Ionian school of philosophy starting with Thales (Gerald Holton)

kakia (plural: kakies) — vice (vices) (Greek)

kensho — initial experience of awakening in which one sees one's true nature (Zen Buddhism)

Ketuvim — sacred text (Judaism)

koan — a paradoxical riddle used to demonstrate the inadequacy of logical reasoning (Zen Buddhism)

laiboni	shamans (Maasai people of Kenya)
the Laylat al Qadr	the "Night of Power and Excellence" in which Muhammad experienced revelations from the angel Gabriel (Islam)
left hemisphere of brain	part of the brain associated with logical, analytical, and verbal skills
li	propriety, that which is proper (China)
limbic system	the emotional brain humans share with other mammals also known as the mammalian brain
logoi	rational principles
logos	reason, rational principle, logic, language, study of (Greek)
the Lyceum	The second known university in the Western world founded by Aristotle
magnum opus	literally "great work" (Latin)
the mammalian brain	the emotional brain humans share with other mammals also known as the limbic system

das Man
"the they," "the one," or "the anyone," (there is no good English translation), the impersonal everyday way of being characterized by conformity to social norms (Heidegger)

manifest destiny
the belief that the United States was destined to expand its dominion across the North American continent

mashiach
messiah, anointed one (Judaism)

the masters of humankind
those who hold significant power and influence such that they drive policy and societal structures to benefit their own interests

materialism
the scientific view that posits that nothing exists except matter and its movements and modifications

the meaning crisis
a perceived widespread decline in the sense of purpose, significance and belonging in modern life (McGilchrist)

meditatio — meditations, ritualized reflections (Latin)

merchants of doubt — individuals or organizations that deliberately sow doubt and confusion about scientific facts to protect their access to profit

metaphysics — inquiry that operates beyond physics (Greek)

metera — mother (Greek)

ming — mirroring of the world (Daoism)

misinformation — false or inaccurate information

moksha — enlightenment (Hinduism)

monogenetic disorder — a genetic condition cause by a mutation in a single gene

monotheism — belief in one God

mountaintop removal — strip mining at the level of mountains

musike — artistic or cultural expression (Heidegger, as interpreted from the Greeks)

narcissism — an inordinate obsession with oneself (psychology)

natura — nature (Latin)

natural selection — the process whereby organisms better adapted to their environment tend to survive and produce more offspring (Darwin)

navi — prophet (male)

Neanderthalensis — the scientific name for Neanderthal, an extinct species of humans

neocortex — the part of the brain where higher cognitive function originates

neuroplasticity — the brain's ability to reorganize itself by forming new neural connections

nevia — prophet (female)

Nevi'im — the words of the prophets (Judaism)

nihilism — a philosophical doctrine that asserts the absence of any ultimate meaning, value, or truth in life

nirvana — enlightenment (Buddhism)

nonlinearity — a relationship or process where a change in one variable does not produce a proportional change in another

noumena — things in themselves (Kant)

nudge — a way to subtly influence people's choices

nutrient pollution — the contamination of air or water with excessive amounts of nutrients (typically nitrogen and phosphorus)

ocean acidification — the decrease of the pH of the earth's oceans primarily caused by the absorption of excess carbon dioxide from the atmosphere

Ockham's razor — a problem-solving principle that advises choosing the simplest explanation from a set of plausible options (William of Ockham)

ontogeny — the branch of biology that studies the development of an individual organism from earliest stage to maturity

ontological dualism — a philosophical framework that posits the existence of two interrelated forces (e.g., yin and yang in Daoism)

ontos — being (Greek)

open system — a system in which the components exchange matter and energy

operant conditioning — a type of learning where behavior is modified through consequences via reinforcement or punishment

orexis — desire (Greek)

paideia — education, informed enculturation (Greek)

paradigm — a model; a set of concepts or thought patterns

paradigm shift — a fundamental change in approach or worldview (e.g., the shift from a geocentric view, with earth as the center, to a heliocentric view of the universe, with the sun as the center; the shift from Newtonian physics to Einstein's relativity and quantum physics)

parameters — the limits that set the conditions of a system's operation

peras — limit (Greek)

persona the public image or social "mask" that an individual presents to the world (Freud)

pesticide a substance used for destroying any living entity deemed to be harmful to agriculture (e.g., insecticides, herbicides)

phenomena appearances (Kant)

phenomenology the study of appearances, the study of the world as it is experienced in context, a philosophical movement founded by Husserl

philia love (Greek)

philosophia The love of wisdom (Greek)

phusikoi naturalists (Greek)

phusis nature (Greek)

phylogeny the branch of biology that studies the evolutionary development of a species

Pithecanthropus Greek name for the first "upright ape man" known now as Homo erectus

poiesis   the bringing forth or revealing of an entity into existence (Heidegger, as interpreted from the Greeks)

polymath   a genius, a person learned in many things (Greek) (e.g., Aristotle, Leibniz, da Vinci, etc.)

positive psychology   field of psychology that studies factors that contribute to human flourishing

pratityasamutpada   the doctrine of interdependent arising (Buddhism) (a.k.a. dependent origination or dependent co-arising)

projection   a defense mechanism in which individuals attribute their own unacceptable or unwanted thoughts, feelings, or impulses onto others (psychology)

propaganda   information of a biased or prejudiced nature, whether disinformation or misinformation, used to promote or publicize a cause or point of view

prophet	one who speaks for god/God
pseudoscience	literally "false science"
psuche	psyche, mind, soul (Greek)
psuche tou kosmos	the soul of the cosmos (Plato)
psuche tou pantos	the soul that permeates all (Plato)
Purusha	the cosmic self (Hinduism)
qi	matter-energy, life force (ancient China)
ratio	logic, reason (Latin)
rational animal	common definition of human being since ancient Greece
rationalism	inquiry that aligns with Cartesian reasoning; philosophical view that regards reason as the chief source of knowledge
rechnendes Denken	calculative thinking that focuses on efficiency, practicality, and manipulation (Heidegger)
ren	benevolence, humaneness (China)

the Renaissance period of Europe roughly spanning the 14th to 16th centuries, characterized by a renewed interest in classical Greek and Roman culture and thought

repression an unconscious defense mechanism where the mind pushes distressing memories, thoughts, or desires out of conscious awareness, thereby protecting the ego from suffering (psychology)

reptilian brain the most primitive part of the brain

respiratory system the network of organs and tissues that work together to facilitate the exchange of gases between the body and the environment

right hemisphere of brain part of the brain associated with creativity, intuition, and spatial awareness

Sachlichkeit a commitment to the things themselves as they are revealed by being (Heidegger)

sapere aude "Dare to be wise," motto of the Enlightenment (Kant)

sapiens — wise (Greek)

Satan — the spirit of evil (Christianity)

Scala Naturae — scale of nature (Latin)

The School of Athens — Renaissance painting by Raphael

self-organization — the process where a system develops order and structure from within

Sein — being (Heidegger)

Seinsfrage — the question of being (Heidegger)

servant leadership — leadership style in which the main priority is to serve the needs of others rather than oneself

the shadow — the unconscious aspects of the personality that are generally deemed unacceptable, undesirable, or negative and thus repressed, denied, or disowned (Jung)

shadow work — psychological practice focused on exploring and integrating the shadow

shalom — peace (Judaism)

Shared Socioeconomic Pathways (SSPs) — calculated scenarios describing potential developments that could impact climate change mitigation and adaptation depending on how humans respond

siduan — the four incipient tendencies of the heart-mind (compassion, shame, respect, and the discernment of right and wrong) (Confucianism)

sinology — the study of China

The Sixth Extinction — current status of biosphere in which species are dying off at a rate that exceeds the natural background extinction rate (term popularized by Kolbert)

social media — websites and apps that enable users to share content and participate in social networking

social media influencer — an individual with a significant online presence who can influence the opinions or behaviors of others

sophia — wisdom (Greek)

sophistry — falsity disguised as truth

sophos — wise (Greek)

the spectacle — a social phenomenon in which everything is presented as a mediated representation rather than as it is in itself (Debord)

le spectacle de l'excès — "the spectacle of excess," a theatrical presentation that emphasizes the exaggeration of gestures, emotions, and roles (Barthes)

Spiritus Sanctus — active presence of God in the world (Christianity)

STEM — Science, Technology, Engineering, and Mathematics

Sterbliche — mortals (Hölderlin)

strip mining — the removal of soil and rock in order to extract coal

subliminal messaging — stimuli presented below the threshold of conscious awareness

subject — "thrown under" (Latin)

summum bonum — highest good (Latin)

sunyata — emptiness (Buddhism)

superego — the aspect of the psyche that harbors internalized moral standards and ideals (Freud)

survival of the fittest	a common description of Darwin's natural selection coined by Herbert Spencer but corroborated by Darwin himself
sustainability	the ability for a system to tend toward continued existence
sustema	an organized whole that stands together, system
swastika	an ancient symbol in the form of an equal-armed cross misappropriated by the Nazis
symbol	an image that represents something more than its literal meaning (Jung)
symbology	the study of symbols
synthesis	the combination of thesis and antithesis (Hegel)
systemology	the study of systems
tabula rasa	blank slate (Locke)
Taishan	Mount Tai, the holiest mountain in Daoism
Tanakh	sacred text consisting of the Torah, Nevi'im, and Ketuvim (Judaism)

techne — the human way of revealing and bringing forth an entity into being; human poeisis (Heidegger)

technological nihilism — a state where the pervasive influence of technology leads to a leveling of meaning to the world or human existence (Dreyfus)

telos — end (Greek)

terra-transformation — the transformation of the earth toward human interests

terra precarium — literally "precarious earth," dangerous terrain

thaumazein — wonder, curiosity (Greek)

thesis — that which is posited (Hegel)

thumos — spirited desire (Greek)

tian — the ultimate reality (Daoism/Confucianism)

tianming — the "mandate of heaven" (Confucianism)

tikkun olam — repair of the world (Judaism)

Torah — five books of Moses (Judaism)

Übermensch	the "overman," an ideal human who transcends conventional morality and embraces self-creation (Nietzsche)
the unconscious	the realm of the mind that contains thoughts, feelings, and memories not readily accessible to conscious awareness
unfalsifiability	the characteristic of a statement, hypothesis, or theory that cannot be proven false
the Upanishads	collection of sacred Hindu texts
urbanization	the movement of persons from rural areas to cities
Verhaltenheit	restraint (Heidegger)
Vernichtungskrieg	war of extermination (Hitler)
villain	archetype representing the repressed, darker aspects of the collective unconscious (Jung)
virtus	virtue, excellent trait (Latin)
Weg	way (German)
Wehrmacht	the Nazi war machine

Welt	world as a coherent nexus of meaning (Heidegger)
der Wille zum Leben	the will to live (Schopenhauer)
wu de	the five Confucian virtues (*ren, yi, li, zhi,* and *xin*)
wuwei	"non-action," masterful but effortless action that accords with the *dao* (Daoism)
xiaoren	small person, small-minded person (Daoism)
xin	heart-mind, integrity (China)
xristos	Christ (Greek)
yang	light, active, masculine element (Daoism)
yetzer ha ra	human inclination toward evil (Judaism)
yetzer ha tov	human inclination toward good (Judaism)
yi	righteousness, justice (China)
yin	dark, receptive, feminine element (Daoism)
zaham	anger, wrath (Judaism)
zhe xue	the study of wisdom (ancient China)

zhengming	the doctrine of the rectification of names, calling things by their rightful names (Confucianism)
zhenren	true person (Daoism)
zhi	wisdom (also rendered *zhe*) (China)
ziran	self-so, spontaneously (Daoism)
zoon logon echon	the animal having logos (Greek)

Selected Bibliography

Ames, Roger T., and David L. Hall. "Philosophical Introduction: Correlative Cosmology—An Interpretive Context." In *Daodejing: "Making this Life Significant": A Philosophical Translation*, edited by Roger T. Ames and David L. Hall, 11–54. New York: Ballantine, 2003.

Aquinas, Thomas. *Summa Contra Gentiles*. Translated by Charles J. O'Neil. South Bend, IN: University of Notre Dame Press, 1975.

Aquinas, Thomas. *Summa Theologica*. Claremont, CA: Coyote Canyon Press, 2018.

Arendt, Hannah. *The Origins of Totalitarianism*. Orlando: Harcourt, 1968.

Aristotle. *The Complete Works of Aristotle*. Edited by Jonathan Barnes. Princeton, NJ: Princeton University Press, 1984.

Austin, James H. *Zen and the Brain: Toward an Understanding of Meditation and Consciousness*. Cambridge, MA and London: MIT Press, 1998.

Augustine, Saint. *Concerning The City of God against the Pagans*. Translated by Henry Bettenson. London and New York: Penguin, 1984.

Augustine, Saint. *Confessions*. Translated by Henry Chadwick. Oxford and New York: Oxford University Press, 2008.

Aurelius, Marcus. *Meditations*. Translated by Robin Hard. Ware, Wordsworth, 1997.

Bacon, Francis. *Meditations Sacræ*. In *Meditations Sacræ and Human Philosophy*, 67–71. Whitefish, MT: Kessinger Publishing, 1996.

Bacon, Francis. *New Organon*. Edited by Lisa Jardine and Michael Silverthorne. Cambridge: Cambridge University Press, 2000.

Baldwin, James Mark. "A New Factor in Evolution." *The American Naturalist* 30, no. 354 (1896): 441–451.

Barthes, Roland. "The World of Wrestling." In *Mythologies*, translated by Annette Lavers, 15–25. New York: Hill and Wang, 1972.

Bernays, Edward L. *Propaganda*. New York: Horace Liveright, 1928.

The Bible.

Bertalanffy, Ludwig von. *General System Theory: Foundations, Development, Applications*. New York: George Braziller, 1968.

Bowlby, John. *Attachment and Loss; Volume 1: Attachment*, Second Edition. New York: Basic Books, 1969.

Brentano, Franz. *Psychology from an Empirical Standpoint*. Translated by Antos C. Rancurrello, D. B. Terrell, and Linda L. McAlister, and edited by Linda L. McAlister. London and New York: Routledge, 1973.

Camus, Albert. *The Rebel: An Essay on Man in Revolt.* Translated by Anthony Bower. New York: Vintage, 1956.

Chuang Tzu. *The Book of Chuang Tzu.* Translated by Martin Palmer. New York: Penguin, 2006.

Coldplay. *X&Y.* Capitol. 2005. Vinyl.

Confucius. *Confucian Analects, The Great Learning and The Doctrine of the Mean.* Translated by James Legge. New York: Dover, 1971.

Crutzen, Paul J. "Geology of Mankind." *Nature* 415 (2002): 23.

Crutzen, Paul J., and Eugene F. Stoermer. "The Anthropocene." *The International Geosphere Biosphere Programme (IGBP) Newsletter* 41 (2000): 17–18.

Csikszentmihalyi, Mihaly. *Flow: The Psychology of Optimal Experience.* New York and London: Harper, 1990.

Darwin, Charles. *The Origin of Species.* Edited by Gillian Beer. Oxford and New York: Oxford University Press, 1996.

Debord, Guy. *Comments on the Society of the Spectacle.* Translated by Malcolm Imrie. London and New York: Verso, 1990.

Debord, Guy. *The Society of the Spectacle.* Translated by Ken Knabb. Berkeley, CA: Bureau of Public Secrets, 2014.

Descartes, René. *Discourse on Method of Rightly Conducting the Reason, and Seeking Truth in the Sciences.* Translated by John Veitch. Edinburgh: Sutherland and Knox, 1853.

Descartes, René. *Meditations on First Philosophy.* Translated by Michael Moriarty. Oxford and New York: Oxford University Press, 2008.

Descartes, René. *Principles of Philosophy.* Translated by R. P. Miller and Valentine Rodger Miller. Bloomington, IN: Indiana University Press, 1983.

Descartes, René. *Rules for the Direction of the Mind.* Translated by Harold Joachim. Westport, CT: Greenwood Press, 1979.

Dey, Tom, director. *Jumpman.* Hanover Films, 2024.

Dreyfus, Hubert L. "Nihilism, Art, Technology, and Politics." In *The Cambridge Companion to Heidegger*, edited by Charles B. Guignon, 289–316. Cambridge and New York: Cambridge University Press, 1993.

Dreyfus, Hubert L., and Sean Dorrance Kelly. *All Things Shining: Reading the Western Classics to Find Meaning in a Secular Age.* New York: Free Press, 2011.

Durham, William H. *Coevolution: Genes, Culture, and Human Diversity.* Stanford: Stanford University Press, 1991.

Dylan, Bob. *John Wesley Harding.* Columbia. 1967. Vinyl.

Dylan, Bob. *The Times They Are a-Changin'.* Columbia. 1964. Vinyl.

Emerson, Ralph Waldo. *Self-Reliance and Other Essays.* Eastford, CT: Martino Fine Books, 2018.

Epictetus. *Encheiridion: The Manual for Living.* Translated by George Long. New York: Barnes and Noble, 2005.

Explosions in the Sky. *The Earth Is Not a Cold Dead Place.* Temporary Residence. 2003. Vinyl.

Fazang. *Commentary on the Awakening of Faith.* Translated by Dirck Vorenkamp. Lewiston, NY: Edwin Mellen, 2004.

Freud, Sigmund. *Civilization and Its Discontents.* Translated by James Strachey. New York and London: W. W. Norton and Company, 1961.

Freud, Sigmund. *The Ego and the Id.* Translated by Joan Riviere. New York and London: W. W. Norton and Company, 1960.

Fromm, Erich. *To Have or to Be?* New York and London: Continuum, 1997.

Gandhi, Mohandas K. *The Gandhi Reader: A Sourcebook Of His Life and Writings.* Edited by Homer A. Jack. New York: Grove Press, 1956.

Gautauma, Siddhartha. *Wisdom of the Buddha: The Unabridged Dhammapada.* Translated and edited by F. Max Müller. Mineola, NY: Dover, 2000.

Guignon, Charles. *On Being Authentic.* Abingdon, UK, and New York: Routledge, 2004.

Haekel, Ernst. *The Evolution of Man.* Delhi: Zinc Read, 2024.

Hansen, James. "The Threat to the Planet." *New York Review of Books* 53, no. 12 (2006): 12–16.

Hansen, James, M. Sato, P. Kharecha, D. Beerling, R. Berner, V. Masson-Delmotte, M. Pagani, M. Raymo, D. L. Royer, and J. C. Zachos. "Target Atmospheric CO2: Where Should Humanity Aim?" *The Open Atmospheric Science Journal*, 2 (2008), 217–231.

Hartmann, Eduard von. *The Unconscious: Speculative Results According to the Inductive Method of Physical Science*. Translated by William Chatterton Coupland. New York: MacMillan, 1884.

Hegel, G. W. F. *The Phenomenology of Mind*. Translated by J. B. Baillie. Mineola, NY: Dover, 2003.

Hegel, G. W. F. *The Science of Logic*. Translated and edited by George Di Diovanni. Cambridge University Press, 2010.

Heidegger, Martin. "The Age of the World Picture." In *The Question Concerning Technology and Other Essays*, translated by William Lovitt, 115–154. New York: Harper & Row, 1977.

Heidegger, Martin. *Being and Time*. Translated by John Macquarrie and Edward Robinson. New York: Harper and Row, 1962.

Heidegger, Martin. *Contributions to Philosophy: Of the Event*. Translated by Richard Rojcewicz and Daniela Vallega-Neu. Bloomington and Indianapolis: Indiana University Press, 2012.

Heidegger, Martin. *Discourse on Thinking.* Translated by John M. Anderson and E. Hans Freund. New York, Hagerstown, San Francisco, London: Harper and Row, 1966.

Heidegger, Martin. *Nietzsche, Volume III: The Will to Power as Knowledge and as Metaphysics.* Edited by David Farrell Krell. New York: HarperCollins, 1991.

Heidegger, Martin. "The Question Concerning Technology." In *The Question Concerning Technology and Other Essays,* translated by William Lovitt, 3–35. New York: Harper and Row, 1977.

Heidegger, Martin. "Science and Reflection." In *The Question Concerning Technology and Other Essays,* translated by William Lovitt, 155–182. New York: Harper and Row, 1977.

Heidegger, Martin. *Zollikon Seminars: Protocols—Conversations—Letters.* Evanston, IL: Northwestern University Press, 2001.

Hogenson, George. "The Baldwin Effect: A Neglected Influence on C. G. Jung's Evolutionary Thinking. *The Journal of Analytical Psychology* 46 (2001): 591–611.

Huberman, Andrew D. *Protocols: An Operating Manual for the Human Body.* New York: Simon Element, 2025.

Hume, David. *An Enquiry Concerning Human Understanding.* Edited by Lorne Falkenstein. Buffalo, NY: Broadview, 2011.

Husserl, Edmund. *Logical Investigations,* Second Edition. Translated and edited by Dermot Moran. London: Routledge, 2001.

IPCC. *AR6 Synthesis Report: Climate Change.* Cambridge: Cambridge University Press, 2003.

Jaspers, Karl. *The Origin and Goal of History.* New York: Routledge, 2021.

Jeanmaire, Peter. "Nature—the Supreme Instance." Available at https://www.reason-to-consciousness.ch/.

Jung, Carl Gustav (Ed.). *Man and His Symbols.* New York: Dell Publishing, 1964.

Jung, Carl Gustav. *Memories, Dreams, Reflections*, Revised Edition. Edited by Aniela Jaffe and translated by Richard and Clara Winson. New York: Random House, 1963.

Jung, Carl Gustav. *Psychology of the Unconscious: A Study of the Transformations and Symbolisms of the Libido: A Contribution to the History of the Evolution of Thought.* Translated by Beatrice M. Hinkle. New York: Moffat, Yard and Company, 1916.

Kabat-Zinn, J., and Richard Davidson (Eds.). *The Mind's Own Physician: A Scientific Dialogue with the Dalai Lama on the Healing Power of Meditation.* Oakland, CA: New Harbinger, 2011.

Kant, Immanuel. *Critique of Pure Reason.* Translated by Max Müller. New York: Penguin, 2008.

Kant, Immanuel. *Groundwork for the Metaphysics of Morals.* Translated by A. W. Wood. New Haven and London: Yale University Press, 2002.

Kant, Immanuel. *On History.* Edited by L. W. Beck, and translated by L. W. Beck, R. E. Anchor, and E. L. Fackenheim. New York: Macmillan, 1963.

King Gizzard & The Lizard Wizard. *Omnium Gatherum.* KGLW. 2022. Vinyl.

Kolbert, Elizabeth. *The Sixth Extinction: An Unnatural History.* New York: Henry Holt and Company, 2014.

Kongzi: see Confucius.

Kuhn, Thomas. *The Structure of Scientific Revolutions.* Chicago: University of Chicago Press, 1962.

Lao Tsu. *Tao Te Ching.* Translated by Gia-Fu Feng and Jane English. New York: Vintage Books, 1972.

Laozi: see Lao Tsu.

Led Zeppelin. *Led Zeppelin.* Atlantic. 1971. Vinyl.

Lee, Kwang-Sae. *East and West: Fusion of Horizons.* Paramus, NJ: Homa and Sekey, 2006.

Leibniz, G. W. *Discourse on the Metaphysics and related writings.* Edited and translated by R. Niall D. Martin and Stuart Brown. Manchester and New York: Manchester University Press, 1988.

Leibniz, G. W. *Monadology.* Translated by Lloyd Strickland. Edinburgh: Edinburgh University Press, 2014.

Leopold, Aldo. *A Sand County Almanac and Sketches Here and There.* Oxford: Oxford University Press, 1949.

Locke, John. *An Essay Concerning Human Understanding.* Oxford: Oxford University Press, 2008.

Lorenz, Konrad. *Studies in Animal and Human Behavior.* Translated by R. Martin. Cambridge: Harvard University Press, 1970.

Lovelock, James E. *Gaia: A New Look at Life on Earth*. Oxford: Oxford University Press, 1987.

Lovins, Amory, Hunter Lovins, and Paul Hawken. *Natural Capitalism: Creating the Next Industrial Revolution*. London and Washington: Earthscan, 1999.

Luders, Eileen, Florian Kurth, D. Das, D. Oyarce, M. Shaw, P. Sachdev, S. Easteal, K. Anstey, and N. Cherbuin. "The Inattentive and Hyperactive Brain: Significant Links between corpus callosum features and ADHD Symptoms in Adulthood." *European Psychiatry*, 31, no. 1 (2016): 197–198.

Luders, Eileen, Owen R. Phillips, Kristi Clark, Florian Kurth, Arthur W. Toga, and Katherine L. Narr. "Bridging the Hemispheres in Meditation: Thicker Callosal Regions and Enhanced Fractional Anisotropy (FA) in Long-Term Practitioners." *Neuroimage* 61, no 1 (2012): 181–187.

Lumineers, The. *Automatic*. Utopia. 2025. Vinyl.

Luria, Alexander Romanovich. *Higher Cortical Functions in Man*. New York: Basic Books, 1966.

Machiavelli, Niccolo. *The Prince*. Translated by Rufus Goodwin. Boston: Dante University Press, 2003.

MacLean, Paul D. "On the Origin and Progressive Evolution of the Triune Brain." In *Primate Brain Evolution: Methods and Concepts*, edited by Este Armstrong and Dean Falk, 291–316. Boston: Springer, 1982.

Marley, Bob and the Wailers. *Burnin'*. Island. 1973. Vinyl.

Marx, Karl, and Friedrich Engels. *The Communist Manifesto*. Edited by L. M. Findlay. Orchard Park, NY: Broadview Press, 2004.

McGilchrist, Iain. *The Divided Brain and the Search for Meaning: Why Are We So Unhappy?* New Haven: Yale University Press, 2012.

Mencius. *Mencius.* Translated by D. C. Lau. New York: Penguin, 2003.

Mengzi: see Mencius.

Metallica. *Monsters of Rock Festival.* Tushino Airfield, Moscow, Russia. September 28, 1991.

Needleman, Jacob. "Introduction." *Tao Te Ching.* Translated by Gia-Fu Feng and Jane English. New York: Vintage Books, 1972.

Newton, Isaac. *Philosophia Naturalis Principia Mathematica.* London: J. Streater, 1687.

Nhat Hanh, Thich. *The Miracle of Mindfulness: An Introduction to the Practice of Meditation.* Translated by Mobi Ho. Boston: Beacon Press, 1975.

Nietzsche, Friedrich. *Beyond Good and Evil: Prelude to a Philosophy of the Future.* Translated by Walter Kaufmann. New York: Vintage, 1989.

Nietzsche, Friedrich. *The Gay Science.* Translated by Walter Kaufmann. New York and Ontario, Canada: Vintage, 1974.

Nietzsche, Friedrich. *Human, All Too Human: A Book for Free Spirits.* Translated by Marion Faber and Stephen Lehmann. Lincoln, NE: University of Nebraska Press, 1984.

Nietzsche, Friedrich. *Thus Spake Zarathustra*. Translated by Thomas Common. Amherst, NY: Prometheus, 1993.

Nietzsche, Friedrich. *Twilight of the Idols or How to Philosophize with the Hammer*. Translated by Richard Polt. Indianapolis and Cambridge: Hackett Publishing Company, 1997.

Nietzsche, Friedrich. *The Will to Power*. Translated by W. Kaufmann and R. J. Hollingdale, and edited by W. Kaufmann. New York: Vintage, 1967.

Nishitani, Keiji. *Religion and Nothingness*. Translated by Jan van Bragt. Berkeley: University of California Press, 1982.

Nishitani, Keiji. *The Self-Overcoming of Nihilism*. Translated by Graham Parkes and S. Aihara. New York: SUNY, 1990.

Nishitani, Keiji. "Only a God Can Save Us: *Der Spiegel's* Interview with Martin Heidegger." Translated by Maria P. Alter and John D. Caputo, *Philosophy Today* 20, no. 4 (1976): 267–284.

Oreskes, Naomi, and Erik M. Conway. *Merchants of Doubt: How a Handful of Scientists Obscured the Truth on Issues from Tobacco Smoke to Climate Change*. New York and London: Bloomsbury, 2010.

Ornstein, Robert. *The Psychology of Consciousness*. San Jose, CA: Malor Books, 2021.

Osnos, Evan. *The Haves and Have-Yachts: Dispatches on the Ultrarich*. New York: Scribner, 2025.

Pelluchon, Corine. *Heading Out to Sea: An Ecological Existentialism*. Translated by Philippe Mesly. Cambridge: Polity, 2025.

Petty, Tom. *Wildflowers & All the Rest*. Warner Bros. 2020. Vinyl.

Plato. *Complete Works*. Edited by John M. Cooper. Indianapolis and Cambridge: Hackett, 1997.

Polt, Richard. *The Emergency of Being: On Heidegger's* Contributions to Philosophy. Ithaca and London: Cornell University Press, 2006.

The Qur'an.

Richardson, William J. "Towards an Ontology of Bob Dylan." *Philosophy and Social Criticism* 36, no. 7 (2010): 763–774.

Rockström, Johan, et al. "A Safe Operating Space for Humanity." *Nature* 461, no. 7263 (2009): 472–475.

Rolling Stones, The. *Out of Our Heads*. Decca. 1965. Vinyl.

Schelling, Friedrich Wilhelm Joseph von. *System of Transcendental Idealism*. Translated by Peter Heath. Charlottesville, VA: University of Virginia Press, 1978.

Schönfeld, Martin. "American Disenlightenment: Climate Change Made in the USA." In *Environmental Ethics for Canadians*, Second Edition, edited by Byron Williston. Oxford: Oxford University Press, 2015.

Schönfeld, Martin. "Falling Down a Waterfall: An Examination of Crisis." *Comparative and Continental Philosophy* 9, no. 3 (2017): 260–263.

Schönfeld, Martin. "The Fork in the Road," *Journal of Global Ethics* 14, no. 3 (2018).

Schopenhauer, Arthur. *The World as Will and Representation*. Translated by E. F. J. Payne. Indian Hills, CO: The Falcon's Wing, 1958.

Seneca. *The Stoic Philosophy of Seneca: Essays and Letters*. Translated by Moses Hadas. New York and London: W. W. Norton & Company, 1958.

Shakur, Tupac. *Greatest Hits*. Death Row. 1988. Vinyl.

Skinner, B. F. *The Behavior of Organisms*. Cambridge, MA: B. F. Skinner Foundation, 1991.

Smith, Adam. *An Inquiry into the Nature and Causes of the Wealth of Nations*. Edited by Laurence Dickey. Indianapolis and Cambridge: Hackett, 1993.

Sperry, Roger, M. S. Gazzaniga, and J. E. Bogen. "Interhemispheric Relationships: The Neocortical Commissures; Syndromes of Hemisphere Disconnection." In *Handbook of Clinical Neurology*, edited by P. J. Vinken and G. W. Bruyn, 273–290. Amsterdam: North-Holland, 1969.

Spinoza, Baruch. *Ethics*. Translated by James Gutmann. New York: Hafner Press, 1949.

Stevens, Anthony. *Archetypes: A Natural History of the Self*. New York: William Morrow and Co., 1983.

Stevens, Anthony. *Archetype Revisited: An Updated Natural History of the Self*. New York: Routledge, 2015.

The Tanakh.

Taylor, Charles. *The Ethics of Authenticity*. Cambridge, MA, and London: Harvard University Press, 1991.

Taylor, Charles. *A Secular Age*. Cambridge, MA, and London, England: Harvard University Press, 2007.

Taylor, Charles. *Sources of the Self: The Making of Modern Identity*. Cambridge, MA: Harvard University Press, 1989.

Teilhard, Pierre de Chardin. *The Phenomenon of Man*. New York and London: Harper, 1965.

Teilhard, Pierre de Chardin. *The Divine Milieu*. New York and London: Harper and Row, 1960.

Ten Years After. *A Space in Time*. Chrysalis. 1971. Vinyl.

Thoreau, Henry David. *Walden*. Secaucus, NJ: Longriver Press, 1976.

Tinbergen, Nikolaas. *The Study of Instinct*. Lexington, MA: Pygmalion Press, 2020.

Tool. *Aenima*. Zoo. 1996. Vinyl.

The Tripitaka.

The Upanishads.

The Vedas.

Velvet Underground, The, and Nico. *The Velvet Underground & Nico*. Scepter and Mayfair. 1967. Vinyl.

Watts, Alan. *The Way of Zen*. New York: Vintage, 1999.

White, Lynn, Jr. "The Historical Roots of Our Ecological Crisis." *Science* 155, no. 3767 (1967): 1203–1207.

Wilson, E. O. *Consilience: The Unity of Knowledge.* New York: Vintage, 1998.

Wilson, E. O. *The Future of Life.* New York: Vintage, 2002.

Wolff, Christian. *First Philosophy, or Ontology.* Translated by Klaus Ottmann. Thompson, CT: Spring, 2022.

Zhuangzi: see Chuang Tzu.

www.ingramcontent.com/pod-product-compliance
Lightning Source LLC
Chambersburg PA
CBHW070803160726
48004CB00001B/300